Studies in Child Development

Family Advice
Services

Studies in Child Development

Titles in this series
Four Years On
11,000 Seven Year Olds
Adoption – Facts and Fallacies
Family Advice Services

Family Advice Services

An exploratory study of
a sample of such services organised by
Children's Departments in England

ARYEH LEISSNER, B.A., M.S.W.
Senior Research Officer

The National Bureau for
Co-operation in Child Care

LONGMANS
in association with
THE NATIONAL BUREAU FOR CO-OPERATION IN CHILD CARE

LONGMANS, GREEN AND CO LTD
48 Grosvenor Street, London w1
Associated companies, branches and representatives throughout the world

NATIONAL BUREAU FOR CO-OPERATION IN CHILD CARE
Adam House, 1 Fitzroy Square, London w1

Printed in Great Britain by
Spottiswoode, Ballantyne and Co Ltd
London and Colchester

Contents

Foreword

by the Assistant Under-Secretary of State,
Children's Department of the Home Office

This report by the National Bureau for Co-operation in Child Care records the results of a preliminary study of Family Advice Services undertaken with financial support from the Home Office. It is being made generally available so that local authorities and voluntary bodies can take into account, in their own thinking and planning, knowledge of the variety of approaches being tried out in the pioneer stages of establishing Family Advice Centres.

In 1960, the Ingleby Committee put forward the view that it was the duty of society both to discover families which were experiencing difficulty in bringing up their children, and to help the parents carry out their functions. The Committee recommended that there should be some centre or organisation to which parents knew that they could turn for help and advice – 'some door on which they can knock, knowing that their knock will be answered by people with knowledge and capacity, and with the willingness to help'. Family Advice Centres are a response to this idea, and many local authorities and voluntary bodies – sometimes separately and sometimes in partnership – have been giving it practical expression in ways which reflect their assessments of local needs and circumstances. The time is therefore ripe for a description of this pioneer effort, both to inform further development of the idea and as a means of identifying problems which require study in depth in the wider context of the children's (and family advice) service as a whole.

In carrying out this study on behalf of its member organisations the Bureau has, once again, demonstrated its capacity to achieve the purposes which led to its foundation in 1962. These were to disseminate information, to improve lines of communication between different professional disciplines and between statutory and voluntary services, to encourage development and to further a preventive outlook over the whole field of child care. In less than four years, five major publications have shown the value of the Bureau's inter-disciplinary approach, crossing the boundaries of health, education and social work, and its capacity for objective description of human need and of the response to such need made by a variety of public and voluntary services.

Society is looking to the social services to respond rapidly, and with humanity, to social and economic change which, in scale and speed, has no precedent in recorded history. Change on this scale not only creates new problems; it also calls attention to aspects of human need which previously escaped notice, or could be met without organised social action. But the response must be soundly based on an awareness of real need, scientifically investigated, and met by services which are sensitive, accessible and, above all, acceptable to the people whom they seek to help. This report examines one of the ways in which local authorities and voluntary bodies are seeking to mount such a response. It will be followed by more detailed studies, which will also be carried out by the Bureau with financial support from the Home Office.

Consideration of the broader setting for the work of Family Advice Services must await the recommendations of the Committee which, under the Chairmanship of Mr Frederic Seebohm, is considering the organisation of local authority personal services. In the meantime, however, the work of the Bureau is available to help local authorities and voluntary bodies maintain the momentum of current developments, and see more clearly the nature of the human needs which the services, however organised, must seek to meet.

D. H. MORRELL

Introduction

Background to the exploratory study
By M. L. Kellmer Pringle

This is the first report on the pilot stage of a three-year project on Family Advice Services, which is being financially supported by the Home Office. The Children and Young Persons Act, 1963 makes it possible for local authorities to initiate preventive work so as to make available help to children from socially handicapped families at a much earlier stage than hitherto. Among the ways for doing so, the idea of Family Advice Services has aroused considerable interest; and a number of local authorities are beginning to set up such services. However, there are few models to follow and, indeed, the concept of prevention itself is being interpreted in many different ways. It is likely, therefore, that different methods and structures will evolve, not only because of these differing concepts but also to meet the needs of different localities.

These developments offer an opportunity to do what is all too rarely attempted: namely, to study the aims and effects of a new social service for disadvantaged children and their families from its earliest conception and inception. All too often, the workings and effects of services are examined – if at all – long after they were planned and set up, so that they are likely to have lost their initial flexibility and variability. In addition to the disadvantages of studying a service when it has become 'institutionalised', the opportunity is lost to learn from the 'growing pains' and evolving development of a new service. A historical study, whether of an individual, an institution or a service, is inevitably distorted by factors such as faulty memory, hindsight and unrecorded details.

These considerations led to the proposal to carry out a study of Family Advice Services. By doing so, the Bureau is hoping to be able to make a contribution to the promotion of increasingly family-centred and preventive child care.

The initial phase was conceived as a feasibility study with three interrelated aims: to explore the workings of Family Advice Services as envisaged by Children's Departments, together with the advantages and the difficulties, arising from differently conceived and operated schemes; to develop adequate methods for an operational exercise of this kind; and to find out whether such a study would be welcomed by social work practitioners. In short, the aim of the first phase of the project was to obtain a picture of the present situation.

To this end, information was gathered on a fairly wide, national basis to discover how such services were being planned and how such plans were being put into practice in England. The Senior Research Officer to the study, Mr Leissner, visited sixteen areas, suggested by the Home Office, spending two to four days in each department. In addition, a number of voluntary agencies and Citizens' Advice Bureaux were visited, in order to obtain insight and information which might be of relevance.

The first phase of the study began in April 1966 and a report outlining the main findings was submitted to the Home Office six months later. Because of its topicality and because of the paucity of publications in this area, the Home Office recommended that the report should be published. Before doing so, the manuscript was submitted to all the Children's Departments and other agencies who had collaborated in the work, for their comments and, where need be, amendments. We are very grateful to those who read the draft report critically and made helpful suggestions. Above all, our sincere thanks are offered to the Children's Officers and their staff who, despite the many claims on their time, gave their full co-operation generously and willingly. We also wish to record our appreciation of all the support given to the project by the Home Office which, however, has no responsibility for the views expressed in this volume. Last but not least, credit for unusually speedy publication is due to Longmans who managed to bring out this book within three months of receiving the final manuscript.

1. Aims of the Exploratory Study

The exploratory study set itself the following goals:

a. to provide a description of the trends and patterns which have emerged in practice in a sample group of Children's Departments under the heading of 'Family Advice Services';

b. to gain insight into the situational factors and the attitudes of the relevant personnel which have influenced the crystallisation of the Family Advice Service concept in the above-mentioned departments;

c. to obtain some impressions of the form and direction which the planning for the future development of Family Advice Services is taking, and to gain information regarding needs and expectations relevant to this planning.

Since the Home Office suggested which departments should be visited, it may be assumed that the departments visited by the Bureau's Research Officer constitute a representative sample of those Children's Departments in England who have addressed themselves in one form or another to the Family Advice Service concept. Included in this sample are large cities, medium sized and small towns, as well as rural areas.[1]

In each Children's Department (as well as in the Voluntary Agencies and C.A.B. offices visited) the Research Officer interviewed executive and field staff and was shown F.A.S. facilities. On some occasions group discussions with relevant staff members were arranged. In a few instances the Research Officer talked to staff members in other statutory departments (Health Department, Welfare Department, etc.). In all departments the Research Officer was given access to files and reports dealing with the work of Family Advice Services. We wish to take this

---

[1] In all departments the Research Officer visited several areas or sub-areas. In many cases the same department encompasses rural as well as small and medium sized town settings. Borough Council Departments in the cities usually are responsible for a number of population sectors of different socio-economic and cultural structures.

opportunity to express our gratitude and appreciation to the staff of the Children's Departments, of other statutory agencies, of the voluntary agencies, and the Citizens' Advice Bureaux for their generosity in allocating time and providing information.

The following pages will attempt to provide a general picture of what is actually happening in practice under the heading of 'Family Advice Services' in the visited Children's Departments, as well as to describe the thinking that is going on in this area of endeavour; it is also hoped to throw some light upon the attitudes held by the people involved. Some of the implications of our findings will be discussed later.

It must be stressed that we are, at this stage, only reporting upon tentative findings of a short-term exploratory study. As the very limited time allocated to the Research Officer's visits in each department was not geared to an in-depth study of any aspect of the Family Advice Service Bureaux, we saw no need to identify specific departments in this Report.

It should further be pointed out that we have not, at this stage, sought to obtain information upon attitudes and reactions of F.A.S. clients. Discussion of this subject will therefore be only marginal.

2. Family Advice Services:
General Observations

The Family Advice Service concept is one of the manifestations of the growing awareness of Child Care practitioners and theoreticians that

a. existing conditions demand increasing emphasis upon early preventive services;

b. the prevention of the 'child at risk syndrome', with all that it entails, demands close attention to preventive measures, to counteract or at least compensate for family inadequacies and disruptions.

This awareness led gradually to greater emphasis on preventive social service approaches over and above the traditional rehabilitation and maintenance/repair functions, and to the increased focusing upon the family, rather than the individual child, as the client unit. This orientation, already implemented for some years in many Children's Departments, was given official expression in the Children and Young Persons Act, 1963. As a logical extension of this preventive and family-focused orientation, child care practitioners became alerted to the need for making preventive services easily accessible to families at the earliest possible stage. The recommendation to set up Family Advice Services or Centres gave official formulation to the widely felt need for this type of service.[1]

Official formulation of recommendations for the setting up of Family Advice Services, while based upon the uniformly felt need, differed to some degree in their explicitly or implicitly stated functions and roles. This undoubtedly influenced the direction in which the services developed in practice.

The Oxfordshire County Council Children's Department, for instance, reported:

[1] In fact, advice services of various kinds and under a variety of names had already been set up by a number of Children's Departments before the 1963 Act.

3

'On the more general basis of making available advice, guidance and assistance, the Children's Department since 1952 has been carrying out intensive casework with families and their children living in their homes. The first full-time Child Care Officer to carry a case load of such families was appointed on 1st January 1952, and since then the work has spread and become part of the case load of every Child Care Officer in the Department...'[1]

The implication here is clearly that 'advice' is to be regarded as an aspect of 'intensive casework' and as such, is the function of every Child Care Officer who is assigned to working with families. Our survey found that several Children's Departments do indeed regard the Family Advice Service as an integral part of the Department's casework services. Thus conceived no distinct and specific characteristics of a Family Advice Service can be identified.

A report to the London Borough of Camden General Purposes Committee emphasised the recommendations of the 1960 Committee on Children and Young Persons as follows:

'In 1960 the Committee on Children and Young Persons, under the chairmanship of Lord Ingleby, reported on the steps which should be taken to prevent and forestall the suffering of children through neglect in their own homes. The Committee rightly surveyed a much wider field than the welfare of children, and reached the conclusion that to facilitate the discovery of all families in need of help, there should be some centre or body to which parents and others know they can turn for advice and assistance. The Committee emphasised that in the more densely populated areas particularly there should be some central point which might be called the Family Advice Centre, to which members of the public can turn for advice...'[2]

Stress laid here upon 'the discovery of all families in need of help' has important implications for the formulation of the specific goals and functions of a Family Advice Centre. There is also a hint as to the assignment of priorities for the setting up of such centres ('in the more densely populated areas particularly'). The words 'Parents and others' leave open the question as to what range of clients should be served at these centres. This question has been answered differently in various Children's Departments.

[1] September 1964 *Report to the Secretary of State under Section 1(4), Children and Young Persons Act, 1963*, Oxfordshire County Council Children's Department.
[2] 3 February 1965, Joint Report by the Town Clerk, Medical Officer of Health, Housing Manager, Chief Welfare Officer, and Children's Officer of the London Borough of Camden.

The Children and Young Persons Act, 1963 states under Section I, Part 1:

'It shall be the duty of every local authority to make available such advice, guidance and assistance as may promote the welfare of children by diminishing the need to receive children into, or keep them in care...or to bring children before a juvenile court;...'

The Children's Departments were, of course, guided by this official directive. The conception of the central purpose of Family Advice Services was consequently influenced by the stated focus upon preventing children coming into care or appearing before a juvenile court.

All the Children's Departments we visited have attempted to make constructive use of the recommendation 'that the organisation of preventive work (is) a matter for each authority to decide in the light of their own circumstances'.[1] In all departments Family Advice Service practice, in whatever form, is regarded as a significant and useful aspect of the department's overall preventive effort. In most departments the organisation, staffing, and the provision of facilities of the Family Advice Service have been undertaken in the spirit of the Ingleby Committee Report that 'there should be some centre or body to which parents and others know they can turn for advice and assistance—some door on which they can knock, knowing that their knock will be answered by people with the knowledge and capacity, and with the willingness to help them'.

The above does not contradict the fact that several of the Children's Departments included in our sample did *not* set up a Family Advice Service within, or detached from, the Department. When we found this to be the case, the reasons were due to different constellations of three main factors:

1. The department felt that the functions of easily accessible advice, guidance and assistance were already an integral part of its prevention orientated family casework.
2. The existence of advice centres under the auspices of other agencies seemed to render superfluous the setting up of a Children's Department Family Advice Service.
3. Staff limitations and shortages did not enable the department to assign trained workers to F.A.S. duties.

Three points listed in the Home Office Memorandum of 31 July 1964, in explanation of why 'some authorities consider Advice Centres unnecessary' appear to be valid at the present time. These three points are:

[1] Home Office Memorandum on the Reports of Local Authorities 1 October 1963–31 July 1964.

'1. The community is closely knit, and everyone knows where to turn
   for help or advice;
'2. The Children's Department either at headquarters or in the areas
   already functions as an advisory centre;
'3. Police, clergy, district nurses, welfare officers, etc., are all sufficiently
   well briefed to be able to give any advice required.'[1]

[1] Home Office Memorandum on the Reports of Local Authorities 1 October 1963–
31 July 1964.

3. Types of Family Advice Service Settings

The specific ways in which Family Advice Services have been put into practice by the different Children's Departments seem to have been determined by a number of factors or combinations thereof. These factors are:

a. the definition of the goals and functions of a Family Advice Service.

b. the established or assumed needs of the area's population, and the already existing services which meet these needs.

c. policy decisions of the Local Authorities' Children's Committees.

d. the availability of suitable staff.

e. the kind and degree of co-operation of other statutory and voluntary agencies in the area.

f. the personal initiative of individual staff members of the Children's Department.

We found four major types of Family Advice Service settings:

1. The Family Advice Service as a unit (or staff assignment) within the Children's Department.

2. The Family Advice Service as a unit serving several local and/or statutory agencies.

3. The Family Advice Service under the auspices of a voluntary agency, financed and partly supervised by the Children's Department.

4. The 'detached' Family Advice Centre serving a specific sub-area, neighbourhood or community.

In the following pages we shall discuss briefly the development and present practice of the above listed four types of Family Advice Service as observed in the Children's Department of our sample group.[1]

---

[1] As already indicated, different types of F.A.S. settings were often found in operation within the same County or Borough Children's Department.

3·1 The Family Advice Service as a unit within the Children's Department

Six of the Children's Departments we visited operate a Family Advice Service as an integral unit of the Children's Department. The physical setting usually consists of a waiting room (in some cases serving other department units as well as the F.A.S.) and one or two interview rooms. The facilities are located on the premises of the Children's Department. They are usually situated near the main entrance to the department, and are advertised either by a separate sign at the entrance door or outside the building. These signs either simply state 'Family Advice Service' and give the receiving hours, or else add details such as 'Free and Confidential Advice on Family Problems'. In several cases a sign outside the building reads: 'Children's Department and Family Advice Service'. The appearance of the F.A.S. facilities ranges from spacious, bright, well furnished and cheerfully decorated to somewhat cramped and rather uninviting rooms, furnished only with the barest necessities.

The ideal goal of this type of Family Advice Service setting is, in the words of a report issued by one of the departments, an operation whose 'functions dovetail so neatly into those of the department as to form an integrated and thoroughly desirable whole'.[1]

The degree to which this goal has been reached varies from department to department.

A foster home is needed*

Miss W, an attractive young woman of twenty, came to the Family Advice Service to ask whether a temporary foster home could be found for her illegitimate one-year-old daughter. She explained to the worker that she had met a young man who had proposed marriage to her but posed the condition that her child be put in a foster home until both of them had established a home, and had become financially solvent. The young man had only recently begun in-service training with a large company, and there was a good chance that he would receive an adequate salary within a year or so. She herself had begun to train as a nurse, in order to be able to bring in her share of the family income.

Until now, Miss W had worked as a nurse's aide, and had paid for the child's day-care out of her small salary. The baby's putative father had contributed to the child's keep in the beginning, but

*This is the first of a number of brief case histories to illustrate points made in the text. In order to safeguard confidentiality the Children's Departments who were kind enough to furnish this material have not been identified.

---

[1] Appendix A to Children's Officers' Report on Family Advice Centre, Barrow-in-Furness, 1964.

then emigrated and ceased to meet his obligations. Miss W and her fiancé wanted the baby, but had decided between themselves that it would be best to place the child in foster care for a year, after which they would take her back to live with them.

The F.A.S. worker asked to meet Miss W's fiancé, and explained to both young people the difficulties of finding a suitable foster home, and the complications arising for all concerned, including the child, on placing the baby in foster care and then removing her again after one year.

The Child Care Officer who dealt specifically with such cases was called in and asked for his opinion. This officer suggested that the Children's Department should help the young couple to meet the cost of a day-care arrangement for the child until such time as their combined income enabled them to meet this expense.

Miss W and her fiancé asked for time to think this over, and returned for several additional talks with the F.A.S. worker and the Child Care Officer. They decided to accept the latter's suggestion, but asked that the baby be given into foster care for a period of one month while they found and furnished a new flat, and arranged for the marriage to take place. This was found acceptable, and a temporary home for the child was found.

Miss W and her fiancé got married, and Miss W's little daughter was returned to them. The F.A.S. worker asked one of the Department's Family Care Officers to visit their home to check if any further help was needed. This officer reported that things seemed to be going well with the young couple. The Children's Department helped to find a suitable day-care placement, and shared in the cost for a period of nine months, after which time the young couple were willing and able to fend for themselves.

To an important extent the quality and mode of operation of this type of Family Advice Service are reflected in, and determined by, the system of staffing. A number of differences in approach were found:

In one department a senior Family Caseworker was assigned to F.A.S. work, and exempted from other Child Care duties. This worker maintained his own filing and recording system and was supervised by the Deputy Children's Officer.

In several departments a worker was assigned to F.A.S. work on a part-time basis, and carried an additional case load of regular work, such as family casework, Child Care, adoption, and foster care. Here the recorded material on F.A.S. clients was kept in the files of the Children's Department *per se*.

Child Care and/or Family Case workers from several departments were assigned to F.A.S. work on a rotation basis, so that a number of officers took turns on duty as F.A.S. staff, each officer receiving F.A.S. clients once or twice a week or once in two weeks.

In all departments the receptionist and clerical staff serve the entire department, and are not specifically assigned to the F.A.S. Unit.

In a number of departments an F.A.S. Unit operates on the premises of area or sub-area offices. Here too the Family Advice Service is regarded as an integrated unit in the Children's Department setting. The same distinctions apply as have been pointed out for F.A.S. units located on the premises of the Children's Departments' central offices.

3·2 The Family Advice Service as a unit serving several statutory agencies

This type of Family Advice Service is in operation in two Children's Departments, both functioning in different ways.

The first of these F.A.S. settings is located on the premises of the building in one of the London Boroughs which houses the Children's, Health, Welfare, and Housing Departments. The F.A.S. setting here consists of a receptionist who, after an initial brief interview, refers clients to rotating 'duty officers' of the four departments mentioned above.[1]

A Reception Officer's remarks

It is difficult to generalise about what happens when a client comes to the F.A.S. desk. They all have different needs and problems, and different ways of expressing them. Their initial reactions also vary widely. Some are shy and embarrassed, others distrustful and apprehensive, a few defensive and belligerent. It is only rarely that I meet a client who is calm and confident, and able to state his purpose clearly.

There is one overall rule we apply at the reception desk: We don't ask any unnecessary questions, we don't probe, and we try, as tactfully as possible, to prevent the client from telling us all the things he should be telling the social worker later on.

The reasons for this should be obvious. Most people would resent having to answer questions about their personal affairs, and then being sent on to another official, to be asked the same questions all over again. Moreover, it is awkward for most people to repeat the often somewhat upsetting story of their troubles for a second time, after they have made the effort during their first bid for help.

Some people are misled by the sense of relief they get from unburdening themselves to the reception officer. Their problem has not really been solved, but their anxiety is temporarily allayed and they have lost their motivation for talking to the social worker.

So we try to limit ourselves to asking for the essential information, and to getting just enough facts to be able to refer clients to the

---

[1] The participation of the Housing Department has lately been greatly reduced because of the overwhelming work load of this department's staff.

most appropriate of the four statutory agencies which collaborate
in our Family Advice Service. That is not always as easy as it
sounds. The other day a Child Care Officer complained that a
young woman I had referred to him seemed to have 'talked herself
out' at the reception desk before she came to him. There was nothing
I could have done about this. As usual, I asked for the essential
facts, but the woman's need to get things off her chest was so great,
that short of being rude there was no way of stopping her from
pouring out everything that bothered her.

Much of the work consists of referring a client to the right agency.
That includes explaining carefully why the client is being sent there,
what the function of that agency is, what procedure the client will
have to go through, and, last but not least, exactly how to get there.

For example: a young unmarried mother asked for help because
she found it difficult to bring up her child. I told her about the
day-care facilities available under the auspices of the Health
Department, but had to warn her there were long waiting lists.
I suggested that, if she required full time care for her child, she
should contact the Children's Department. She was given precise
directions how to explore these two possibilities, and asked to return
and let us know what happened, and whether she needed further
help.

Another example: A mother told me that she had difficulties in
controlling her fifteen-year-old daughter, and that her landlord
had evicted her that morning, putting her furniture out into the
street. I gave her three sets of instructions:

a. How to check with the Housing Department on whether the
eviction was legal.

b. How to request assistance from the Welfare Department on the
grounds that she was homeless.

c. How to contact the right person at the Children's Department
in order to receive guidance with regard to her problems with
her daughter.

There is always the danger that a client may feel that he or she
is being 'passed on' because of our lack of interest. Quite a few of
our clients seem to have the experience of being 'shunted about'
from one official to the other when dealing with government
departments.

Despite the pressure of work, one has to remain sensitive to this
feeling, even if it is not openly expressed. A few sympathetic and
understanding words often do wonders in assuring the client that
we are sincerely interested in helping, and that we shall continue to
be available for help, guidance and assistance.

There are, of course, a number of 'regulars' who come again
and again, and who know quite well what they want, and to whom
they wish to speak. These people often stop to chat with me while
they are waiting for their appointment. It is important to make
them feel at ease, but to avoid discussing the cases with them in a
way which might interfere with the treatment plan of the assigned
social worker.

The F.A.S. reception desk is a busy spot in the spacious entrance
hall of the large modern building which houses four statutory
departments. Many people in trouble reach this desk at the end
of a long road of worry and confusion. The reception they find here
may become a turning point in their lives. It is very important that
their many questions be answered clearly and sympathetically and
that they be sent on with the feeling that, from now on, they will
be given the competent professional help they need. That is what
my job is all about.

*Summarised from written communication from the Reception Officer of the
London Borough of Camden Family Advice Service.*

The second F.A.S. setting is the result of a Local Authority decision
in a rural and small town area. Here a policy decision to integrate the
services of the Children's Department and the Welfare Department
brought about the setting up of a Family Advice Service Centre in one
small town, staffed by officers of both departments. The clerical staff
serves both departments, and a common card index system is maintained. Although the goal of this particular setting is an integrated
Family Advice Service pooling the resources of the two participating
departments, it appears (as expressed by the staff) that both departments
function in fact as separate units, each offering advice services
according to the statutory duties and working condition of its own
service. This, it is thought, will continue while the two local authority
services remain unintegrated and responsible to different spending
committees.

3·3 Family Advice Services in the voluntary agency under Children's Department auspices

Two Children's Departments have financed (on the authority of the
Children and Young Persons Act, 1963) the setting up of Family Advice
Services in local Settlement Houses or community centres.

In both cases the Children's Department pays the salary of an F.A.S.
worker who, while receiving guidance and some degree of supervision
from a senior Child Care Officer, is directly responsible to the director
(Warden) of the voluntary agency. These Family Advice Centres
are regarded as part of the service provided by the settlement
house or community centre to the population of a specific
neighbourhood. Office space was made available on the premises of the
agency.

A marriage beyond repair

Mrs T, a young Cypriot, came to the Family Advice Service of a small Settlement House in an urban area in an obvious state of agitation and distress. She had left her home, with her two children, after a fight with her husband, and spent the night in the flat of a friend. A neighbour who had made use of the Family Advice Service some time ago had advised her to see the F.A.S. worker.

Mrs T said that she needed somewhere to live, as she could not continue to impose upon her friends. What she told the worker about her marriage, involving a long history of violent quarrels, court summonses, and heavy drinking by the husband, convinced the worker that Mrs T could not return to her home in the present circumstances.

The F.A.S. worker telephoned the Welfare Department to ask for their co-operation in finding accommodation for Mrs T and her children. The Welfare Officer contacted Mrs T's husband immediately, and prevailed upon him to vacate the flat and leave it in Mrs T's possession. Mrs T and her children returned to their home that same afternoon.

The following day the F.A.S. worker had a long talk with Mrs T, to help her arrive at some long-term plans regarding her marriage. The worker contacted the local matrimonial court in order to obtain factual information. He advised Mrs T to see the solicitor whom she had engaged some months ago in the matter of a court summons against her husband. The solicitor proved reluctant to pursue the matter, and agreed to assist Mrs T only after several weeks of negotiation.

In the meantime Mr T had disappeared, and the court was unable to serve a summons upon him. During this time the F.A.S. worker saw Mrs T regularly, and, in a series of casework sessions, helped her to view her situation realistically and to cope with her emotional distress.

Eventually Mr T was located, and a court order was obtained. The F.A.S. worker discussed the situation with both parties, and helped them work out a mutually acceptable arrangement which permitted Mr T to visit his children from time to time.

3.4 Detached Family Advice Centres

This type of Family Advice 'outpost' has been set up in several Children's Departments; one of them in a large city and others in mixed rural and small town areas.

In all cases this type of Family Advice Service was initiated in response to a growing awareness of the need for such a service in specific high-problem sectors of a given area. We noted three variations of this type of service:

a. Family Advice Centres set up in facilities provided by other statutory
agencies (Health Clinics, Infant Care Centres, Probation Departments) in high-problem areas of a large city or small town. These
advice centres, open to the public one to four afternoons and/or
mornings per week, were staffed either by a specially assigned part-
time worker, or by rotating Child Care Officers, who also carried
regular case loads. In all these cases it was not clearly distinguishable
whether the Family Advice Centre had specific functions to perform,
or whether it constituted mainly a kind of sub-sub-area office of the
Children's Department.

Repairing a broken marriage

Mr I, aged forty-eight, a skilled welder earning about £25 a week,
came to the Family Advice Centre because, after prolonged crisis,
his world had finally collapsed.

Mr I told the worker that his wife and four children, aged six,
eight, thirteen and seventeen, had left him to live with his married
daughter (aged twenty-two) in the north of the country.

Mr I was extremely concerned for the welfare of his wife and
children, who, as far as he knew, had no means of support. He was
certain that their moving into his married daughter's house would
cause extreme overcrowding as well as financial hardship.

A solicitor had advised Mr I to refrain from giving material help
of any kind, pending a legal decision. Mr I was so distressed that
he broke down and cried several times during the interview. His
presentation of the problem was confused and erratic, and it took
all the worker's skill to obtain a clear picture of the situation.

The worker made no attempt to probe into the past, or to imply
any blame. His understanding, accepting attitude put Mr I at ease
and, in the course of a series of talks, made him receptive to the
worker's advice as to practical steps which might repair the damage.

Mr I was gradually enabled to face his own inadequacies as
husband and father. He admitted that he had spent a dispropor-
tionate amount of his income on alcohol, and that this was one of
the major reasons for the breakdown of his marriage. Somewhat
more at peace with himself, and resolved to do everything possible
to make amends, Mr I, with the worker's guidance, wrote to his
wife and pleaded with her to return. With his agreement, the
worker also sent a letter to Mrs I to assure her of Mr I's sincerity.
He also contacted the Children's Department in Mrs I's present
locality, to initiate home visits by a local Child Care Officer, and
to obtain for Mr I a reassuring report regarding the welfare of his
family.

Meanwhile, Mr I co-operated in a series of intensive casework
interviews aimed at enabling him to gain insight into his personal
problems. The need for medical treatment became apparent, and
the worker contacted Mr I's physician with regard to this.

Mr I visited his family in the north country three times in order to maintain contact, demonstrate his concern, and discuss a possible solution. These visits, and Mr I's newly gained self-assurance and rational attitude, led to a reconciliation.

Mrs I and her four children returned home. The worker visited the family shortly after her return, and gained the impression that the relationship between Mr and Mrs I had sufficiently improved to offer hope for their future. Casework continued with both parents and with their full co-operation. The goal is to help them to a correct view of their respective roles, to enable them to function more effectively, to consolidate their reunion, and to help them come to terms with recent events.

b. Three detached Family Advice Centres differed from the above operation mainly in their greater emphasis on focusing upon community problems.

Two of these were set up in new industrial towns largely inhabited by predominantly unskilled or semi-skilled immigrants employed and housed by local industry. The Family Advice Centre here had its own facilities, sharing the premises with other statutory and voluntary agency staff, such as the Welfare Department, the Health Visitor, the Mental Hygiene Clinic, and Citizens' Advice Bureau, the Family Planning Clinic, Moral Welfare, N.S.P.C.C., Catholic Welfare, and the Family Service Unit. Here, too, the distinction between regular Children's Department work and specific F.A.S. functions is not clear. However, the specific and numerous problems (mainly debts and marital conflict) abundant in this community geared the work of the Family Advice Centre to a special emphasis which was not felt to the same degree in the regular work of the Children's Department.

Another Advice Centre of this type operates in an overspill area of a small town, populated by an influx of working-class population from one of the neighbouring large cities. Here the Family Advice Centre immediately responded to a number of glaring community problems. The assigned officer first and foremost became active as a community worker and, backed by the Children's Department, initiated community action, such as forming a Tenants' Association, as well as becoming instrumental in effecting such changes as the reduction of rents by the local Council.

c. In one London borough the Children's Department rented a flat in a block of tenement houses populated almost exclusively by slum clearance, multi-problem families. A staff member was assigned to maintain a Family Advice Centre in this flat. This worker carried no other duties in the Children's Department, and worked under the supervision of a senior Child Care Officer. Responding to the pressing community problems clients brought to her in the course of their making use of the Advice Service, the worker initiated and supported community action on such issues as playgrounds for children, improvement of repair services, cultural activities etc. While continuing to provide assistance and advice within the statutory limits of the Children's Department, this Family Advice Centre became in fact a community service.

A detached Family Advice Centre

Having selected a densely populated building in a low-income housing estate as the site for a pioneering attempt at establishing a 'detached' Family Advice Centre, the Children's Department instructed the appointed F.A.S. worker to make a three-months' exploration of the needs, resources and characteristics of the inhabitants.

During this period a wealth of information was gathered on the eighty or so families who had recently been rehoused from a slum area and now lived in the selected building; contacts were also established with the staff of the numerous statutory and voluntary social agencies who worked in the area. This done, the Children's Department rented a two-room flat in the building, and the worker tacked a sign to the door which said in bold letters:

CHILDREN'S DEPARTMENT
FAMILY ADVICE CENTRE
OFFICE HOURS MONDAY/FRIDAY
1 p.m.–5 p.m.

During the first week the Centre remained empty, and Mrs M, the F.A.S. worker, began to feel somewhat frustrated and lonely.

The following week she spent some time during the mornings wandering through the building, knocking on doors, and introducing herself. She told people about the new Family Advice Centre, and explained its functions. The response she found ranged from enthusiastic welcome and non-committal politeness, to puzzled shrugs and a curt, hostile 'I'm very busy, I can't be bothered'.

That week Mrs M left the door to her office wide open, and settled down behind her desk to await developments.

Soon some of the children of all ages who were playing noisily on the staircases and the landings came in to stare at the 'new lady'. For the next few days these children were her only visitors. They asked for a drink of water, and used the toilet, flushing it enthusiastically. They tried the chairs, and leafed through the magazines which had been provided. They used Mrs M's pen to scribble on the stationery, and discovered the uses of the stapler. Mrs M, herself a mother of three active youngsters, bore this patiently, with a friendly word for the little ones and an occasional chat with the older children.

Then, one afternoon, an apologetic mother came in. She wanted to know if her children were making a nuisance of themselves. She accepted the offer of a chair and a cup of tea, and stayed to chat about herself and her neighbours. This lady, or else the children, spread the word that there was a telephone in the office, the only one in the building. Soon people came to ask whether they could make a call. They were readily given permission, and often stayed to talk.

Almost two weeks after the opening of the centre, just as Mrs M was getting ready to go home, a man walked in, and said: 'My wife told me that you can help people with problems. Now I have a little trouble, and wanted to ask you what to do about it.'

Mrs M opened a drawer of her brand new filing cabinet, and took out one of the folders. Her first client had arrived.

4. Goals and Functions in Theory and Practice

We have advisedly included 'goals' and 'functions' under the same heading because, as in so many other areas of social work practice, we cannot always be certain which of the two classifications suitably describes our subject matter. Nor is it always possible to decide what preceded what: were the functions of the type of social work which we offer under the heading 'Family Advice Services' derived from a set of clearly defined, preconceived goals, or did the goals take shape, and become tangible in response to, and as a result of, clusters of functions which accumulated more or less accidentally beneath the F.A.S. label?

In the following pages we shall try to afford the reader some insight into this question as it pertains to our subject, by brief discussions of the following questions:

1. What goals have been set for the Family Advice Services?
2. What are the basic definitions upon which these goals rest?
3. What functions were assigned to the Family Advice Service, and what are the practical applications of these functions?

4·1 The goals

As already indicated in the introductory remarks, the Family Advice Service concept can be regarded as one of the facets of the crystallisation of what we may call the prevention goal, which was given official recognition and status in the Children and Young Persons Act, 1963. More specifically applied to the Family Advice Service this overall goal of prevention narrows down to two closely related target areas:

a. the prevention of family breakdown (or, in another formulation, the prevention of families becoming 'families at risk'), and

b. the prevention of children coming into care and/or appearing before a juvenile court.

Those two, closely related, major goals, which were set for the Family Advice Service, gave birth to two derivative goals, which can also be regarded as descriptive of the main functions of this service:

18

c. the provision of an easily accessible, easy to use source of competent advice, guidance, and assistance to *all* families in need of this type of help;

d. the earliest possible detection of children and families 'at risk', preferably *before* the 'at risk' stage has been reached.

In the course of our study it became apparent that these two last mentioned goals may under certain circumstances, and in certain of their aspects, become incompatible.[1]

Two additional goals, which seem to have grown spontaneously out of the practical experience of F.A.S. staff, came to our attention. One of these may be called the initiation and improvement of field level co-ordination between the staff of the relevant statutory and voluntary agencies. The second is the provision of a community service (in distinction from a family service) to foster and improve community relations and community action.

4·2 Definitions

For obvious reasons, we cannot go fully into the definition of 'prevention', a major concept with decisive implications for the entire field of social welfare. It must suffice here to point out that the term, while taken for granted, appears not to have been clearly defined by the professional practitioners involved in the Family Advice Service. As a recent report stated: 'This word prevention still has much to teach us, official and voluntary agencies alike. The boundaries of prevention and the details of preventive work, are by no means clear.'[2]

The difficult age

Mr L, an impressive-looking, heavy-set man in his forties, had difficulty in finding the right words to tell the F.A.S. worker what was bothering him. He said that he had read the advertisement about 'Free and Confidential Advice in all Family Problems' in the local newspapers. He didn't think he really had a problem; it was just that he wanted to talk to 'someone who knows about psychology'.

Mr L was a foreman in a car factory. He had an adequate income, was happily married, and father of three children. He had always thought that he was 'a good father' but lately he didn't seem to be able to get on with his oldest son, a boy of fifteen. Terry had always been a 'good boy'. He had done well at school, was obedient, and helpful around the house. During the last few months the boy

---

[1] This point will be discussed in more detail when we deal with the problem of possible conflict between statutory child care and Family Advice Service functions.

[2] Cambridge House Annual Report 1965, London Borough of Southwark.

seemed to have changed. Not that he was doing anything really 'bad', but he had become sloppy in his appearance, left his things lying about, on occasions came home late from school. What was even more upsetting, the boy had begun to 'talk back' to his father, and Mr L had caught him lying.

Mr L seemed to be a straitlaced, somewhat rigid man of strong convictions, though not unkindly and with a sense of humour. The F.A.S. worker found it not difficult to put him at his ease and establish a friendly relationship. As it happened, the worker himself had some experience in dealing with teenagers. He asked Mr L to tell him what he thought his reaction to the boy's behaviour should be. Mr L said that he was not at all sure, but thought that it might be best to 'tighten the reins'. Perhaps he had been too lenient, and should impress upon his son that he would not tolerate any kind of bad behaviour. He had never found it necessary to hit the boy, but if he didn't 'straighten out' physical punishment might become necessary.

The F.A.S. worker did not argue with him. Instead, he began to talk in easily understandable terms about that 'difficult age' of adolescence. He told Mr L about the physical and emotional changes of puberty, of the need felt by adolescent youngsters to assert their budding independence, and how this often found expression in odd behaviour, deviousness, and open rebellion. He talked about the decisive influence of peers at this age, and how important it became not to be treated as a child any more, while, on the other hand, there was considerable anxiety over having to face the responsibilities of manhood.

From his own experience with teenagers, the worker recalled stories of typical teenage behaviour, almost always rather disturbing and puzzling to parents. Soon Mr L chipped in with some stories of his own, and he and the worker found themselves chuckling together over some of the more bizarre antics of adolescent youngsters.

Mr L seemed much relieved. It seemed, after all, that Terry was not turning into a monster, but was going through a normal phase of development, characteristic of his age. Without the worker's prompting, Mr L concluded that it would be wrong to 'come down heavily' on the boy, and that an over-punitive attitude might well endanger his relationship with Terry, and make the youngster even more rebellious. The kid might even seek relief from an oppressive atmosphere at home in bad company on the street.

Mr L said that he understood the situation much better now, but he had not known enough about this before.

The worker talked a bit about the need for 'setting limits' at this age, and how this could be done with understanding, and without turning the relationship between father and son into a 'war between the generations'.

Mr L left, having thanked the worker and told him that he might come in again for a chat if he felt that he needed additional advice.

The F.A.S. worker, catching up with his paper work, felt that this had been an hour well spent. As Terry had not done anything which would have warranted Mr L seeking the intervention of any other agency, such as the Probation Department, or Mental Health Clinic, the Family Advice Service had been the right place, and perhaps the only place, to come to. The advice and reassurance Mr L had received may very well have prevented a serious deterioration in his relationship to his son, and a crisis in Terry's development.

Our observations have shown that, in practice, the concept of prevention is as loosely and widely, or as narrowly, applied as the individual worker deems fit. The 1963 Act itself seems to permit a very wide range of discretion in this area. In more concrete terms, a shiftless, unstable and unhappy young man in his early thirties, without family, may be accepted as a client by a Family Advice Service worker because offering him constructive help in one or several areas of his life, may prevent him from becoming a future source of family conflict (if he marries or has 'at risk' children in or out of wedlock). On the other hand, a mother of several children, whose family life shows no overt problems, and who comes in to chat, fulfilling a vaguely felt need to 'have a talk with somebody', may be discouraged from continued use of the worker's time because preventive work does not seem to be indicated.

Perhaps equally significant is the fact that the boundaries between 'prevention' and 'rehabilitation' are not, and perhaps cannot be, clearly drawn. One of the most important practical results of this is that F.A.S. staff usually carries a mixed load of preventive and rehabilitation cases. This lack of distinctions, perhaps fully justified by practical experience, adds to the widespread blurring of the differences between the regular work of the Children's Department and the specific functions of the Family Advice Service. This is especially so, as all Children's Departments we have visited regard preventive work as part of their regular duties. As a Home Office Memorandum pointed out: 'Local Children Authorities have a duty under Section I of the 1948 Act to aim at the restoration to their family of children who have been received into care; and in a number of areas the family casework carried out for this purpose was developed into work to prevent family breakdown.'[1]

We ran into even more difficulties with the term 'advice', a key word in the Family Advice Service concept. Here too, the interpretation and application of the term is left largely to the worker's discretion. Specifically, F.A.S. staff has found it problematic to decide whether the

[1] Factual Memorandum by the Home Office on the Local Authority Children's Service in England and Wales, February 1966.

simple and direct provision of information and 'one-shot' advice without any further implications should be included in the definition of this term. In many instances 'advice' has actually been interpreted as meaning casework, and work with clients who ask for 'simple advice' is regarded as of secondary importance and as time-wasting.

A Case of 'Simple Advice'

Mr C, a factory worker, father of three children, took an hour off from work to come to the Family Advice Centre to ask whether there was a way in which he could return several pieces of furniture obtained on hire purchase. He said he didn't like the way they were made.

The worker briefly explained hire purchase regulations. Mr C thanked him, but the worker had the impression that the man remained apprehensive and unconvinced. Mr C answered further questions evasively, and departed abruptly in what appeared to be a state of great anxiety.

Two months later Mr C returned to the Family Advice Centre accompanied by his wife and children and asked whether he 'could have a talk'. After a few opening remarks, Mrs C took over, and said that she and her husband could not agree upon how their money should be handled and how to repay their mounting debts. She said that she was on the verge of leaving Mr C because of this, that her physical health was deteriorating, and that her family doctor had recommended that she see a psychiatrist.

The interview soon showed that excessive hire purchase commitments and other debts that she had made without the knowledge of her husband were the basis of this family's crisis. The C's had now received a number of court summonses, and a notice on rent arrears from the Housing Authority. At the worker's request Mrs C produced all her bills and accounts. The total debts amounted to well over £400. The weekly earnings of Mr C, including overtime, averaged £14 to £15 a week.

The F.A.S. worker took immediate steps to help Mr C negotiate the return of a number of the recently purchased items to the respective stores, thereby reducing the overall debt to approximately £300. The worker then helped Mr C to obtain an Administrative Order from the local County Court.*

Since then the assigned case worker has helped Mr and Mrs C to 'work through' the marital problems arising from their financial

* An Administrative Order is a procedure in which the applicant applies for a Court Order against his own person with regard to the total sum of his debts. The court is empowered to order the applicant to pay off his debts in regular instalments according to his income and ability as evaluated by the court. Creditors are obliged to comply with this order. The applicant is bound over not to incur further debts until he has paid off in full. Payments are made to the court or to an appointee of the court, who distributes them to the creditors.

difficulties, and to devise and maintain a sensible system of budgeting. A series of individual counselling sessions with the worker have helped Mr C to adopt a more active role in the financial management of his family, and to understand more fully the weaknesses and needs of his wife. The C's family life has greatly improved, and this case can now be regarded as closed, although the worker continues to be available for guidance and advice.

The manner in which the term 'advice' has been defined has had important implications in two areas:

a. the crystallisation of unique functions for the Family Advice Service, distinct from those of the regular duties of the Children's Department;
b. the distinction between the functions of the Family Advice Service and the work of other agencies, such as the Citizens' Advice Bureaux.

4.3 The functions assigned to the Family Advice Service

A number of questions concerning the functions of the Family Advice Service are being asked in the field; some of them have found answers in practical application, others have remained open. We shall list the most important of these 'functional questions' and discuss them briefly:

1. Who are the people who are in fact, or should be, served by the Family Advice Service? This question poses a number of other, related problems, such as:

a. Are there significant differences in the need and the actual demand for this type of service by the different socio-economic and socio-cultural population groups?
b. Should there be an allotment of priorities to one or another socio-economic strata of the population?
c. What are the criteria for making the Advice Service available? Should the F.A.S. client be a member of a family which includes children, or can he be a single, unattached individual, or a member of a childless family? Or is it sufficient that he is a member of a community which a specific Advice Centre has made its focus of attention? Should F.A.S. service be offered mainly to those who are *not* in contact with any other social agency?

A new immigrant seeks help

Mr S, a recent immigrant from India asked the Family Advice Service worker to help him find more suitable employment. The man's family was still in India. He had been employed as personnel manager in one of India's biggest firms, and was now working as an unskilled labourer in a factory.

Although Mr S's attitude was reserved and uncomplaining, he was obviously unhappy about the situation. It became clear to the worker that Mr S's low income and the loss of status he felt as a result of having to do work which was far below his qualifications, had led to a marked lowering of self-esteem. This situation also had made Mr S reluctant to undertake practical steps to have his family join him in England.

As a first step to helping Mr S shake off a growing sense of isolation, and to enable him to regain a measure of self-confidence and hope, he was given the opportunity to join a social activities group of the local neighbourhood association, and to participate in a series of evening seminars dealing with cultural topics.

A few months after his first contact with the service, Mr S felt sufficiently confident to enrol at the local university for evening classes, and to initiate steps to have his family join him. In the meantime the worker is making every effort to help Mr S find a more suitable and satisfying job, but so far these efforts have not met with success.

2. How 'aggressive' should the Family Advice Service be? Is it enough to make the service accessible and available, or should clients be 're-cruited' by giving the service wide and effective publicity, or even through actually knocking at the client's door?

3. Is 'reaching the unreached' one of the F.A.S. functions? Is there a need for this function (are there, in fact, 'unreached' families, in-dividuals, or population groups in the area)?

Who are the 'unreached'?*

Multi-problem families. There is a certain type of multi-problem family which poses special problems for preventive work in the form of advice, guidance and assistance. Such families often have a long history of severe emotional strain. They are prone to severe anxiety, and fits of depression. Their defensive mechanisms include a wide variety of antisocial behaviour, expressed in delinquency, inept handling of financial obligations, inadequate housekeeping, excessive drinking, sexual promiscuity, and aggressive behaviour towards neighbours. More often than not they refuse to co-operate with social workers and administrators who represent authority. They are particularly crisis-prone, using the crisis situation as a sort of safety-valve which permits them to ward off anxiety and depression, and to express openly their diffuse anger.

They rarely seek help for their emotional problems, but are

Summarised from written communications from the staff of the County Borough of Preston, and the Devon County Council Children's Departments, and from the field notes of the Senior Research Officer.

notorious scroungers and frequent callers at agencies which provide material aid. If they accept professional help at all, it is usually on the condition that their demands for material aid be met unconditionally. Although these people often exasperate the worker by their incessant demands, their dishonesty, and their skill at manipulation, they, perhaps more than anyone, need carefully planned and patiently given help.

Because of the overwhelming problems they pose, helping agencies more frequently accede to their demands for material aid, rather than provide the long-term, in-depth treatment which is needed.

Fringe groups. In many areas there are population groups, such as new immigrants, (West Indians, Africans, Indians, Irish, Cypriots etc.) and vagrants and tinkers, who tend to remain on the fringes of society, and lead a relatively isolated existence. In many cases the language problem adds to their difficulties. The members of these groups are often frightened and confused. They are most likely to react to their environment with fear, distrust and hostility, and to their own condition with apathy or despair.

Many of these people are unable to make effective use of the benevolent but multifaceted and complex services and institutions our society provides. They don't know where to go with their problems, and even when they have found the right address, they are often unable to express themselves adequately or to understand the directives they are given. Without adequate, systematic help their situation is most likely to deteriorate further. Those few of them who, due to above-average personal resources, or by sheer luck, succeed in making adequate adjustments, leave their inferior environment. A hard core of down-and-outers remain behind. Such groups present a challenge which the understaffed and over-burdened helping agencies are often unable to meet.

Men who live on their own. There are a great number of men who, having left their parental home, have not founded families of their own. Their very condition is an odd and problematic one in a society in which it is expected of the male adult that he assumes the responsibilities of founding and maintaining a family. A significant number of these men, especially in the lower classes, lead frustrated, shiftless lives, beset by emotional and financial trouble. Some of them live in lonely isolation, others congregate in groups of their own kind, some are vagrants. There seem to be no helping agencies whose services are geared to reaching these men and rendering them adequate assistance. Many of them are fiercely independent, and reluctant or unable to establish relationships, accept obligations and face responsibilities. This may lead to antisocial attitudes and behaviour, and makes it all the more difficult to provide them with professional guidance. Some of these men turn to alcohol and sexual adventure to allay their anxieties and to ease their loneliness. A great number of illegitimate children are fathered by men of this kind. A 'safe', confidential, 'no-strings-attached' advisory service may very well be the best answer to the special needs and characteristics of these men.

Women alone. Experience seems to show that women who stay unmarried and live by themselves in adult life are more likely to make adequate adjustments than men in similar circumstances. It also seems that society does not consider the unmarried female as odd as her male counterpart. Nevertheless there are a significant number of middle aged unmarried women who feel that they have no one to turn to in times of need. Emotional problems are frequent and, as in the case of the solitary male, the existing helping agencies do not seem to be geared to providing adequate services.

The teenagers. Despite the widespread belief that there is a proliferation of services for teenagers, there is considerable evidence that many boys and girls in the 16–21 year age range are acutely aware of having no one to turn to when they are in need of advice, guidance and help.

A boy may have become greatly concerned with some of the more disturbing side-effects of his physical growth; he may be self-conflicted about his choice of career, his relationship to his peers, or his involvement with a girl; he may suspect a venereal infection, or feel trapped because he has drifted into drug addiction.

A girl may have become anxious about her appearance, her popularity, the company she keeps; she may feel rejected or imposed upon by her parents; she may be disturbed about a sexual experience, an incident of petty theft, or the marihuana cigarette she smoked at a party.

In a great number of such instances, the youngster is thrown back on his or her own meagre resources, and the questionable advice of peers. The youngster either doesn't know of any competent, understanding person in whom he or she could confide, or is prevented from seeking the help of an adult by fear, shame, guilt, distrust or resentment of authority.

An Advisory Service geared specifically to the need of teenagers might prove invaluable. Such a service will have to make a special effort to assure the youngsters of a matter-of-fact, non-judgmental and strictly confidential attitude. The professional staff will have to be selected with special attention to their ability, their 'talent' to understand young people and their problems and to establish the kind of relationship of trust and respect which is the essential prerequisite for competent and fruitful work with teenagers.

4. Is the 'detection' of problems a major function of the Family Advice Service? Should the service be geared to detecting children and/or families 'at risk', or limit its service to dealing with the 'presented' problems?

'I think I ought to see a lawyer'

A rather upset elderly gentleman came to the Family Advice Service office, and said: 'I don't know if I'm in the right place, I think I ought to see a lawyer, but maybe you can help me.'

He told the worker that he and his wife lived in a first floor flat nearby, and had been bothered to the point of distraction by the loud stamping, running and scraping that went on above their heads day in, day out. A family lived in the flat above them who apparently had no consideration for other people. They were a young couple who left the house early in the morning and returned in the late afternoon. Their three children, aged two to five, stayed alone in the flat, and made an inordinate amount of noise. The old gentleman had tried to reason with these people. At first they promised to silence the kids, but the noise went on unabated, and when he remonstrated with them again, they became impertinent. The old gentleman had complained to the landlord, but the latter had taken no action.

'My wife and I are in our late sixties,' the man said, 'We are not well, and spend most of our day at home. We need a little peace.'

The F.A.S. worker, while sympathetic to this elderly couple's plight, was even more concerned with the fact that three very young children were apparently left alone in an empty flat throughout the week. She immediately brought the case to the attention of the Children's Officer, and a Child Care Officer visited the flat of the young couple that evening. Without identifying the complainant the officer explained to the parents that their behaviour was not only inconsiderate, but in fact an infringement of the law.

The young couple were duly impressed, but said that they had no alternative, as they both held jobs, and could not make ends meet on just one salary. The Child Care Officer replied that nevertheless, a solution had to be found, as it was his duty to take statutory action if they continued to leave the children unattended.

In the course of several meetings with the young couple, it was agreed that the mother of the three children would change to half-day employment. The F.A.S. worker was able to locate a nearby family who were willing for a modest remuneration, to look after the children until their mother returned from work.

5. What range and depth of service can the Family Advice Service offer? Is 'simple advice and information' a waste of the worker's time? Must a client become a 'case'? Should the F.A.S. worker offer the same service as any other Child Care Officer or Family Case worker employed by the Children's Department (supervision of children at risk, family casework, material assistance)? Should the Family Advice Service

initiate and/or operate auxiliary services such as play groups, holiday camps, clubs? Do the functions of the F.A.S. staff include such activities as group work and community organisation work?

6. What are F.A.S. functions in relation to other statutory and voluntary agencies? What are the criteria and limitations for accepting referrals from other agencies? To what extent does the Family Advice Service function as a 'clearing house' and referral service for other agencies? Can and should a Family Advice Service assume co-ordinating functions?

1. *Who are the people served by the Family Advice Service?*

All Family Advice Services visited by the Research Officer stated that the majority of their clients come from the lower and working-class segments of the population. In several areas with sizeable concentrations of immigrant groups (Indian, Pakistani, West Indian, African, Cypriot, Irish, etc.) a significant proportion of the F.A.S. clientele came from these population groups. In a number of areas, containing inhabitants from several socio-economic strata, F.A.S. staff reported an increase of clients of middle-class backgrounds. This was especially pronounced in one of the university towns.

A Marriage in Danger

Mr and Mrs B came to the F.A.S. office and came straight to the point:

Both were agreed that they needed advice in dealing with their mounting marriage difficulties.

Mr B was recently qualified as a civil engineer, and Mrs B, aged twenty-one, appeared also to be well educated. The B's had one child.

The F.A.S. worker noted from the outset that Mr and Mrs B were ready and eager to discuss their problem. They showed a certain amount of insight, and expressed themselves well and intelligently. The overt manifestations of the marital conflict were clearly stated during the first interview:

Mrs B reacted with apparently irrational anger and panic whenever her husband went out without her. In subsequent talks with the F.A.S. worker Mrs B related her present difficulties to the extremely unhappy marriage of her parents, who separated when she was eighteen. Mrs B had made a suicide attempt at the time.

The F.A.S. worker consulted the Medical Social Worker where Mrs B had received psychiatric treatment after her suicide attempt. In joint consultation with the Medical Social Worker, the F.A.S. worker broached with Mr and Mrs B the possibilities of referral for psychotherapy or to a Marriage Guidance Clinic.

> The B's, however, decided to try a change of environment first,
> and went abroad to live with Mr B's family. All other plans are now
> held in abeyance, and it is expected that Mr and Mrs B will resume
> their contact with the Family Advice Service if they feel that the
> new situation has not solved their problem.

In several departments the obvious preponderance of need among the
lower-class and working-class population led staff to assign priorities of
service to the aforementioned groups; however, this remains purely
theoretical, since in practice there is no discrimination of any kind in
serving clients of whatever background.

In some departments staff stated the need for a concerted effort to
make the advisory services more attractive and accessible to middle
class clients. The reasons given were:

a. that many middle-class families were not receiving preventive help
because they regarded the social services as mainly intended for the
lower socio-economic strata of society;

b. that a significant proportion of middle-class people in the F.A.S.
clientele would serve to remove the stigmatising image of the service
as one used mainly by the failures and the destitute of society.

All F.A.S. staff we interviewed expressed the opinion that the function
of the service is to serve people in need of advice, guidance and assistance,
regardless of their socio-economic or cultural background.

The question of whether the Family Advice Service should be limited
to families with children, or whether it should serve any individual, is a
more complex one. In most departments this particular issue has been
decided with reference to the statutory functions of the Children's
Department. Here the Family Advice Service only accepts clients who
present problems in which children are directly or indirectly affected.
In a few exceptional cases F.A.S. staff has, in practice, served single
individuals, married couples without children, and elderly couples
whose children have left home. In these latter cases no policy decision
was made and workers used their own discretion.

A man alone

Mr A wrote to the Family Advice Service at the suggestion of his
doctor. He stated that, although a skilled worker, he could only do
light casual work because of a chest ailment. In order to obtain
such work in his own trade it was necessary for him to become a
member of the appropriate Trade Union and be placed on the
Union's register.

Despite long negotiations and protracted discussions the Union, while accepting him as a member, insisted on registering him for regular work. Mr A tried full-time work, but collapsed and had to leave.

Upon receipt of Mr A's letter, the F.A.S. worker visited Mr A at home to discuss his situation with him in more detail. Following this, the Family Advice Service enlisted the co-operation of the local Labour Party. The F.A.S. worker found out that the Party officials had dealt with Mr A's case eighteen months previously, but were not aware that the situation had not been alleviated. An official visited Mr A at home, and a member of Parliament made representations to the Union on his behalf.

Mr A's case has not yet found its final solution. However, he knows that practical steps are being taken to help him, and there is every reason to hope that before long his requirement will be adequately met.

In all departments there is some concern about this question. In some instances staff have challenged the views of the term 'family' advice service, and expressed their feeling that the limitation to families with children was 'unfair' in that it excludes a large number of potential clients.[1] This issue poses less of a problem in the Family Advice Centres which were set up within a specific community and focused upon the community *per se*, and upon community problems.

In all Family Advice Service settings we have seen, clients are accepted regardless of their contact with other agencies. In fact, a great majority of clients are already involved with one or several statutory or voluntary agencies at the time they seek F.A.S. help.

'Everyone knows the Green family'

A tired and exasperated Health Visitor was sitting across a desk from the Family Advice Service worker. She had come to ask whether the F.A.S. worker could have a look at the Green family. 'Everyone knows that family,' the Health Visitor said, 'but no one seems to have found a solution for them.'

She reported briefly what she knew of the Greens:

The family lived in a council flat which had steadily deteriorated during their tenancy, and was now in an advanced state of neglect. Mrs Green, a thirty-year-old woman, worn out by having given birth to five children, and after an unknown number of mis-carriages, had long ago given up any attempt to keep the house

[1] It may be of some interest here to note the following statement in a recent magazine article which discusses the work of the Seebohm Committee: 'The Committee itself is interpreting "Family" liberally enough to include one-person households and wandering alcoholics' (*New Society*, 8 September 1966, p. 368).

tidy, although she was an affectionate mother and her children were relatively well cared for. A timid woman, of low intelligence, Mrs Green now lived in fear of another pregnancy, and this had begun to affect her relationship with her husband.

Mr Green, a small, rather gentle man, seemed very fond of his children and his wife, but was unable to cope with the responsibilities his steadily growing family imposed. Physically weak, he had never held a job longer than a few months, and usually was laid off either because he complained that the work was too hard, or because he stayed away from work to take care of his family during his wife's frequent periods of illness.

The Health Visitor saw the family frequently, and it was largely due to her efforts that the children were reasonably well clothed and fed. The School Welfare Officer had arranged free meals for the school-age children, and had visited the family at home. As the Greens had fallen behind with the rent, the Housing Department had become involved, treating them with commendable patience and forbearance. The National Assistance Board had made extra payments on several occasions of emergency. A voluntary church agency in the neighbourhood had taken an interest in the family and, on occasion, provided them with secondhand furniture and items of clothing. A volunteer worker from this agency visited the home from time to time to have a chat with Mrs Green.

After an initial visit to the Green family's home, during which the F.A.S. worker made sure that they were willing to accept her help, the worker met with the officials of all the agencies which had become involved, in order to discuss the situation. Everyone contacted seemed only too glad to have the Family Advice Service take an interest in this family.

It became quite clear that a long-term, supportive casework relationship was needed, a service which none of the other agencies could provide.

The F.A.S. worker visited the Green's home at regular intervals. In addition to this, Mr and Mrs Green came to the Family Advice Service office from time to time to talk over specific problems.

Arrangements were made with the School Welfare Officer to have the older children continue to get their dinners at school during the holidays. A grant for clothing, blankets, and some necessary items of furniture was obtained from the Children's Department. The latter also helped to arrange for a badly needed two-weeks' holiday for Mrs Green and her two youngest children. The F.A.S. worker prevailed upon the local council to assign a Home Help for the Greens.

In co-operation with the Health Visitor, Mrs Green was provided with medical treatment to alleviate her run down physical condition, and the F.A.S. worker accompanied her to a Family Planning Clinic where she was fitted with an intra-uterine contraceptive device.

Having freed Mrs Green from some of the worst immediate pressures, relieved her of her fear of another pregnancy and helped her to

gain a measure of confidence, the F.A.S. worker could enable her
to become more effective in keeping her home in order.

It proved more difficult to bring about a change in Mr Green's
poor work habits. However, after some time had passed, he too
seemed to take a new lease on life, and has now managed to hold
down a job for six months.

Work with this family continues, and the F.A.S. worker intends
to maintain a consistent helping relationship with the family for
some time to come.

The statement in a report on the Children's Department-financed
Family Advice Centre maintained by a Settlement House reflects the
generally accepted view. The report states that it is the function of the
Advice Centre 'to help those who are not known to, or have fallen
between, the social services available, and to give guidance in deciding
who can give them the most positive support'.[1]

2. How 'aggressive' should the Family Advice Service be?

Opinions on this differ to some degree between and within the departments. Some regard it as sufficient to establish the Family Advice
Service in an easily accessible location. Others feel that F.A.S. work
should aim at establishing the kind of image in the area which will gain
the confidence of the population and encourage wide use of the service.
In some departments emphasis is put upon publicising the advisory
service through newspaper advertisements, posters, distribution of
printed cards and circular letters to other statutory agencies, general
practitioners, churches, etc. In several departments, however, executive
staff have refrained from advertising the service due to the fear that this
might lead to an influx of clients which could not be handled by the
limited available staff.

The kind of 'reaching out for the unreached client' which actually
leads the worker to knock on doors in order to offer and explain his
service is implemented only in those Family Advice Centres which
have been established as 'outposts' within a specific community.

3. Reaching the unreached

In all the departments visited it became apparent (and in some instances
was explicitly stated) that the staff is aware of the existence of one or
several population 'pockets' which, for a variety of reasons, do not
receive the help they need. This situation was found to exist in certain

---

[1] Initial Report on the Family Advice Service by the Warden of Cambridge House,
Borough of Southwark, London, undated.

housing estates and in slum areas of large, medium and small towns, populated by new immigrants, slum clearance, or 'overspill' population groups, as well as in some isolated villages in rural areas.

The reaction to this by Children's Department staff differed. In many departments it was felt that future planning of Family Advice Centres should give priority to reaching this type of client. Others suggested that a more effective system of publicising the available service might 'bring in' clients from such unreached groups. In some departments Family Advice Service outposts were established within, or in close proximity to, such areas of isolation. The reaction of a few executive staff members is illustrated by the remark of one Area Officer: 'If there are pockets of unreached people, we don't want to know about it at this stage. We would not have the staff to deal with them.'

On a different level, which touches upon fundamental concepts of social service, several staff members raised the question whether a policy of aggressive reaching out to induce people to seek or accept advice, guidance or assistance, might conceivably encourage an already prevalent tendency to hand over one's problems to the state. This would serve to reduce further the competence of people to solve their own problems, as well as to lessen the incentive for mutual aid within the community.

Many staff members seek to refute this view on the grounds

a. that there is no evidence to show that significant numbers of people have been induced to become over-dependent upon outside help due to the easy availability of social services. On the contrary, there is some empirical evidence that a significant proportion of those who are beset by social, economic and emotional problems are reluctant to make use of the available services;

A difficult client

The Family Advice Service worker of a Settlement House in an urban area received a call from a local School Welfare Officer. A Miss Y had requested free school dinners for her illegitimate daughter. An income statement was required in order to assess the validity of this request, but Miss Y had met all attempts to obtain such a statement with evasion and hostility.

The F.A.S. worker called on Miss Y and obtained the statement after having established a friendly relationship with her. While dealing with this matter, the worker noted the highly inadequate living conditions in Miss Y's flat, and her obvious state of depression. Miss Y complained about the dampness in her flat, and expressed her anxiety over the health of her second child, an infant, also illegitimate.

A series of home visits and talks with Miss Y showed that she was not interested in being helped to take practical measures to get rid of the dampness, but that she had contacted the Housing and the Health Departments to demand a new, and better, apartment. Her behaviour at these agencies, where she made hysterical scenes, and threatened to desert her children, had antagonised the officials.

She inhabited a council flat, and infringed upon the rules by having a man, Mr V, living with her. She had also refused to comply with the Health Visitor's request to take her baby for treatment to the Health Clinic.

Entering a long-term casework relationship with Miss Y, the F.A.S. worker gradually gained her confidence. She became able to talk about her own attitudes, and gained some perspective on her behaviour. It became apparent that one of the main causes of her anxiety and resultant hostility was her feeling of being stigmatised as an unmarried mother, and the disparaging attitude of her neighbours caused by the presence of Mr V in her flat. She regarded Mr V as her common law husband, and wanted to move to a neighbourhood where she had relatives and friends.

The worker had several talks with Mr V, who proved co-operative and showed a sincere and responsible attitude in his relationship to Miss Y and her children.

The worker, in co-operation with the Health Department, initiated negotiations with the Housing Department to obtain Council housing for her in a neighbourhood which she preferred. Shortly before her move, Miss Y took her baby to the Health Clinic for treatment.

When she and Mr V moved into the new flat, the living situation was regularised through the inscription of Mr V's name on the rent book. Hereafter Miss Y called herself Mrs V.

After the family had moved to their new flat, contact with the Family Advice Service ceased.

b. that theoretical knowledge, practical experience and common sense, all lead to the conclusion that people who receive competent professional advice, guidance and assistance regarding areas of imbalance, disruption or pathology which affect their normal functioning, are usually enabled to make better use of their own resources, to adopt a more confident attitude towards problem-solving, and to deepen their understanding of the social value and inherent emotional satisfactions of helping others.

Several Children's Officers have expressed the opinion that it seemed especially difficult to 'reach' the 16 to 21-year-old age group. Many practitioners are convinced that new approaches and methods of service are needed which are especially adapted to the norms and the needs of adolescent and young adult.

One Children's Department has recently taken part in the setting up of a voluntary Young People's Consultation Centre, which includes two physicians in its staff, and tends to emphasise advice on sexual problems.[1]

4. 'Detection' as an F.A.S. function

The issue of the detection of children and/or families 'at risk' as a function of the Family Advice Service has been the subject of discussion in many departments. Generally shared conceptions of the statutory duties of Children's Department staff strongly indicate that any staff member assigned to the Family Advice Service is under obligation to be alert to any indication that children are 'at risk' in the presented problems which clients bring to him.[2]

One F.A.S. Report, for instance, states that 'The Centre has proved enormously valuable as an early warning system of families "at risk"...' (54 out of 127 cases).[3]

One Area Officer stated categorically that F.A.S. staff must be held responsible for using the relationship with the client to identify cases of children 'at risk' and bringing these to the attention of the Children's Department.

In practice most F.A.S. workers use their own discretion in determining the degree to which they will put pressure upon the client to disclose possible existing or potential 'at risk' situations. Difficulties arise, where a client presents a problem which, on the surface, is not related to children, and refuses to respond to probing questions by the worker as to whether a child's wellbeing may not actually be involved. The client may, for instance, ask for advice with regard to an accumulation of debts, and resent being questioned about the effect the resultant tension and anxiety in the home has upon his children. Some workers feel, in such cases, they are obliged to press the point. Others hold that the client's wish to limit his request for help to the presented problem, should be respected. Workers have expressed the opinion that it is more important to create the image of a 'safe' 'no-strings-attached' worker-client relationship in the Family Advice Service setting, than to identify an 'at risk' case. Reasons in support of this view are:

[1] In one medium-sized town a voluntary organisation set up a Young People's Advisory Service, which has a 24-hour telephone answering service. A considerable number of teenagers of both sexes have made use of this service, presenting a wide range of problems. The local Children's Department has not participated in this venture.
[2] This obligation is not felt as strongly in those Family Advice Centres which, while financed by the Children's Department, operate under the auspices of a Settlement House or Community Centre.
[3] Children's Officers' Report on Family Advice Service, Barrow-in-Furness, 1964.

a. the client's possible feeling of having been 'trapped', and his voicing
of distrust and resentment among friends and neighbours, which
may discourage others from using the service.

b. there are sufficient other statutory and voluntary officials (Child
Care, Probation, Police, N.S.P.C.C. officers, Health Visitors etc.)
whose duties include the detection of children 'at risk' or of situations in which children may be 'at risk'.

5. *Range and depth of the services offered by the Family Advice Service*

At first glance the range and kind of help offered by the Family Advice
Service under the heading 'advice, guidance and assistance' appears to
be practically unlimited. An official directive authorises 'the provision
of such advice, guidance and assistance as will serve to diminish the
need to receive children into, or keep them in, care, or to bring them
before the court'.[1]

While this seems to set clearly defined, though broadly conceived,
limits to the functions of the Family Advice Service, it was found that
in practice, the help offered frequently transcends these limits. The
conceptions leading to this are reflected in the statement by the Association of Children's Officers:

'Some families cannot be fitted for a normal life in the community by
grants of material aid, or by the work of services that are concerned
only with one aspect of their problems. They must in a sense be
"converted" to a new way of life. The only means yet discovered for
doing this is the personal influence of someone prepared to help them
in every way that is needed.'[2]

The following list of the specific problem areas in which two Family
Advice Services gave assistance during one year of operation may serve
to provide a representative sample of the types of cases handled by all
the F.A.S. settings visited by the Research Officer.[3]

Children at risk	Matrimonial difficulties
General family problems	Illegitimate pregnancies
Death in the family	Husband in gaol

[1] Factual Memorandum by the Home Office on the Local Authority Children's Service
in England and Wales, February 1966, p. 1.
[2] *Evidence to the Committee on Local Authority and Allied Social Services*, The Association of
Children's Officers, April 1966, p. 4.
[3] The nomenclature is that used in the Reports of the Children's Departments. The
items listed have not been arranged according to their frequency of occurrence.

Housing
National Insurance
Family law
Debts
Unruly neighbours
Employment
Child minding
Adolescent maladjustment
Non-support by husband
Rent, rates, fuel, arrears
   (hire purchase)
Lack of play facilities for
   children
Friction with statutory and
   other officials

Aged parents
Burial charges
Pre-marital problems
Social inadequacies
Criminal law
Alcoholism
Rehabilitation, of mentally or
   physically handicapped
Birth control
Inadequate housekeeping
Lack of cultural facilities
Inadequate sanitary conditions
Budgeting
Removal problems

Although statistics are not available at this stage, the consensus of opinion of F.A.S. staff indicates that child-rearing problems, marital conflict, and debts (especially hire purchase bills, and rent arrears) are the three main problem areas in which clients seek F.A.S. help. Inadequate housing makes a close fourth. The Children's Officer's Report (June 1966) in one large city states: 'Problems presented have concerned poor home conditions (approximately half of the total); children beyond control; youths who do not work; financial mismanagement; advice on adoption and boarding out; and admission enquiries.'

The apparent preponderance of requests for advice, guidance, and assistance in the four problem categories mentioned may be of considerable significance for the operation of Family Advice Services. There are important implications here for the delineation of F.A.S. functions, for the training requirements of staff, and for the co-ordination of services with other agencies. However, the impressions conveyed here remain tentative, and statistical evidence will have to be produced before any conclusions can be drawn.

In any of the problem areas listed above the service offered may range from a brief, informal chat (to help the client abreact some of the tension and gain a new perspective on his problems) to intensive, long-term casework. The F.A.S. worker may initiate a series of marriage guidance sessions, or have several talks with one or more members of the family. The worker may help a client find suitable employment, or assist in working out a family budget. He may intercede on the client's behalf with a hostile neighbour, the Housing Manager, or an N.A.B. official. In some cases F.A.S. workers have taken on the task of weekly rent collection, in order to prevent clients from spending the rent money before it is due. The Family Advice Service may provide a Mother's Help or baby sitter, or prevail upon the relevant authorities to set up supervised playgrounds. In all these cases the overt, presented needs of the client and the worker's diagnostic insight into the underlying problem interact to varying degrees with the worker's own special skills and talents to produce the resulting service, and to mould the client–worker relationship.

'Do you know where I can find somewhere to live?'

Mrs F, a mother of three children came to the Family Advice Centre to ask for help in finding temporary accommodation. She said that she had recently arrived in the town and was, for the moment, living with a relative. She indicated vaguely that she was married, and needed a place to live for a short time only.

Mrs F's physical appearance, threadbare coat, ill-fitting dress and worn-down shoes, suggested that she was hard up. The child with her was dirty, his hair matted, his feet in tattered sandals. He was pale and timid, and clung to his mother during her talk with the F.A.S. worker.

Having obtained the most basic information from Mrs F, the worker asked her about her other two children, her reason for coming to this area, her financial situation and her husband. At first Mrs F seemed reluctant to reply, but after some hesitation and a few evasive answers she suddenly said quite calmly:

'Oh well, I suppose if I need help I had better tell you that I am living with another man, not my husband, and that it is his sister I am staying with, and she wants us out of her front room as soon as possible.'

Mrs F told the worker that the man she lived with now was unemployed, and his only resources consisted of some money left over from National Assistance payments received in the town he came from.

Talking about her problems, Mrs F gradually became more relaxed, and soon was pouring out her troubles. She told of her separation from her husband, and dwelt at length upon her uneasy, conflict-ridden relationship with the man with whom she had been living for the last year. This man and Mrs F had left their previous abode and come to this area after having been evicted and having accumulated a great many debts. It also became apparent that Mrs F had badly neglected her health and was in need of medical attention.

Shortly after Mrs F's first interview at the Family Advice Centre, the F.A.S. worker visited her at her temporary address. What he saw there led him to have the youngest child, aged two received into care immediately. Four days later the worker was able to secure adequate provisional accommodation for Mrs F and her family. A monetary grant was provided to purchase the most essential furniture, and the youngest child was returned to Mrs F.

It is now a little over two years since Mrs F came to the Family Advice Centre to ask where she could find a room. She and her children have been on the case list of the F.A.S. ever since.

Her common law husband served a prison term during these two years, and after his release the family returned to their town of origin. Within a few months they were back, and a fourth child had been added to the family. They found accommodation, but were evicted for non-payment of rent and because of the aggressive attitude of the man. The case worker assigned to the family found them a large comfortable flat and mobilised the resources of the community to help Mrs F furnish it. Even so, the situation deteriorated further, and when Mrs F became pregnant again her four children had to be received into care until after she had given birth.

The social worker assigned to this family persisted in his efforts to persuade Mrs F's common law husband to assume responsibility for the upkeep of the family. This met with failure, and the burden of maintaining the family continues to be borne by the National Assistance Board.

Mrs F and her children were enabled to use the facilities of the Children's Departments' Day Training Centre for Mothers. This centre includes a play group, and makes a concerted effort to teach the mothers budgeting, dressmaking, cooking, etc., as well as affording them the opportunity to relax, emerge from their isolation, and gain insight into their problems through group experience and through scheduled talks with the case worker.

Under the guidance of the Family Advice Centre, Mrs F has now applied for a divorce and has taken steps to arrange for maintenance payments from her husband. The case worker visits Mrs F's home at regular intervals and reports that the physical care of the children has greatly improved, and that Mrs F now receives the medical attention she needs.

The oldest of the children is attending school and a vacancy in one of the local nursery schools was found for one of the other youngsters.

The family continues to be on the 'at risk' case file. The children are, however, well cared for now, reasonably clean and adequately clothed, and, as far as circumstances permit, Mrs F is a good mother to them.

It has for instance been observed that a worker who received special training in marriage guidance work emphasised this aspect of his service to clients. Another worker, with a community organisation background, tended to focus upon community action solutions. This factor will have to be taken into consideration in meeting the training requirements of F.A.S. staff, be that in the form of courses and seminars, or in the planning of overall social work curricula.[1]

1 See further discussion of the training implications under the topics 'staffing' and 'planning for the future' in Chapters 5 and 6 respectively.

4

As an integrated or detached unit of the Children's Department, the Family Advice Service can, where circumstances warrant this, provide financial assistance under Section 1 of the Children and Young Persons Act, 1963. All F.A.S. settings we observed offer such financial assistance in the form of grants, or loans in cases of debts, rent, rate or services arrears, fares, removal costs, and household necessities. In a number of cases Children's Department funds are supplemented by donations from voluntary agencies. There appears to be no questioning of the relevance and usefulness of this type of assistance. It is, however, not always clear whether financial assistance should be made available directly through the Family Advice Service, or whether the client should be referred to the Children's Department in cases where material aid is indicated. Most departments take the latter course. In some instances F.A.S. staff may provide financial assistance directly, but in consultation with the senior officer in the department.

Paying the rent

Mrs G, a widow with three children, came to the Family Advice Centre after she had been evicted from her flat for non-payment of rent. The F.A.S. worker's investigation showed that Mrs G is an adequate, responsible mother, who found it extremely difficult to make ends meet on a widow's pension.

Mrs G had located a flat at a rent she could afford, but was unable to pay the two weeks' rent in advance requested by the landlord. The worker, making use of funds available to the Children's Department under the Children and Young Persons Act, 1963, provided Mrs G with a grant to cover the two weeks' rent advance. This money was paid directly to the landlord.

As Mrs G's deceased husband had been an ex-service man, the worker contacted the British Legion and S.S.A.F.A. on her behalf and they agreed to pay her rent arrears in full.

Mrs G gained new confidence and courage through the understanding attitude and the constructive aid given her. With the additional help of the worker's guidance and advice, she learned to cope with her financial difficulties and to maintain a satisfactory home for her children.

In addition to the question of the range and type of services to the client that are to be included in the functions of the Family Advice Service, the issue of the quality, depth, or intensity of service has been raised. The problem can be summed up in the question: '"Simple advice", "Intensive casework" or both?' In most F.A.S. settings we have seen, the answer to this question appears to be: Both (simple advice as well as intensive casework), **and** all possible variations thereof, including an empirically developed form of short-term counselling, are made available.

Flexibility in this area is made easier by generally accepted, rather broad definitions of 'intensive casework', as exemplified by the following statement, which defines intensive casework as: 'A professional social work relationship in which very frequent and regular contact between the social worker and the client is aimed at producing a greater feeling of confidence and competence on the part of the client.'[1]

'Simple advice'[2] has caused F.A.S. and Children's Department staff some unease. One of the reasons for this is that the trained worker frequently feels that giving one-shot answers to simple requests for instruction or information constitutes a trivial and uneconomic use of the worker's skill and time. A strong additional argument against providing 'simple advice' is that there are other agencies (especially the Citizens' Advice Bureaux) who have this function. On the other hand staff members contend that the F.A.S. worker must be ready to allot a good part of his time to this type of service, if the Family Advice Service is to become broadly accepted and widely used by the population. Moreover, these officers feel that many clients tend to 'test' the service repeatedly with simple, and perhaps rather trivial, questions, before they have gained enough confidence to present more complex and anxiety-producing problems.

'Can you give me your opinion?'

Mr D presented a picture of a deeply troubled man when he came to the Family Advice Service. He was faced with a difficult decision and wanted the worker's opinion on what was the right and what the wrong thing to do.

Mr D's 23-year-old unmarried daughter had become pregnant. A man of strong moral principles, Mr D was shocked and angry, and his first reaction was that it was his duty to turn the girl out of his house. His wife had taken her daughter's side, and had threatened to leave him if he did so.

Mr D was willing to accept the worker's judgment, and wanted a straight answer: Was it 'right' or was it 'wrong' to renounce his erring daughter? The F.A.S. worker acknowledged Mr D's urgent and immediate need by answering him directly. She said that, in her opinion, and based on her experience of the consequences, it would be wrong to evict the pregnant girl from the house. Mr D thanked the worker, assured her that he would take her advice, and left.

---

[1] Barbara J. Kahan, *The Work of the Children's Care Committee and the Children's Department*, Oxfordshire County Council, May 1965.
[2] This is the term used in the Children's Departments.

Six months later Mr and Mrs D came to the F.A.S. office with their infant grandson. Their daughter, the child's mother, had left home and deserted the baby. The D's said that they needed help, but were not able to express clearly just what kind of help they were seeking at the moment.

A series of home visits, and a number of consultative talks with several other social workers from other agencies, who had become involved with the D family, brought forth a picture of a complex and unhealthy situation.

Mrs D was considered an inadequate mother, and Mr D had a history of mental illness. Two of the D's children were on probation, and a third had been sent home on trial while still subject to a 'fit person order'. Mr D had been accused of an incestuous relationship with the daughter who had left home, as well as with the younger, 13-year-old, girl.

In the course of an investigation, Mr D was cleared of this charge, and his 18-year-old son admitted that it was he who had sexual relations with his sisters, and that he was the father of the older daughter's baby. Subsequently the 13-year-old girl was removed from home under a 'fit person order'.

In consultation between the F.A.S. worker and the many social workers from other agencies who were dealing with the D family in various capacities, it was decided to reduce the number of workers, thereby arriving at a more sharply focused treatment plan for this family. The D family was referred to the Mental Welfare Department for treatment and supervision.

In most departments F.A.S. staff is, in fact, discouraged from providing 'simple advice', and where such advice is given it is usually not recorded. The most frequently cited reason for this is that the questionnaires of the Home Office pertaining to F.A.S. work exempts 'simple advice' from its area of interest. Cases 'in which only the giving of simple advice and information were required' are specifically excluded from the required statistics in the relevant questionnaire.[1] The same circular states 'Applications for references which were disposed of without investigation, e.g. by the giving of simple information or by re-direction, to another department or agency, need not be counted'.[2]

Additional questions which have arisen are whether the functions of the Family Advice Service should include

a. the operation of auxiliary services, and

b. activities which can be regarded as community organisation and group work.

The first question (a. above) has been answered affirmatively in

[1] Home Office Circular No. 66, 1 June 1966. Appendix B.
[2] Ibid. Appendix C.

several departments. Here it was felt that it was entirely within the functions of the Family Advice Service to set up and supervise Mothers' Clubs, Play Centres, Vacation Camps, budgeting and housekeeping courses, etc., where a significant number of clients have expressed a need for such services. The staff of one Family Advice Centre in a voluntary setting has suggested the setting up of English language classes, and the recruitment of volunteer interpreters, for the many new immigrants with language difficulties who live in this particular area. In some cases F.A.S. staff has been instrumental in initiating the setting up of these kinds of services by other agencies, such as Housing Departments, Park Departments, Settlement Houses, etc., in some instances financing these projects with Children's Department funds under Section I of the 1963 Act. We found no opposition to this type of activity. Where such projects were not set up, the reason was mainly that either there seemed to be no need for them, or else they were sufficiently provided by other agencies.

The second question (b. above) is a somewhat more controversial one. While not stating any outright opposition to this idea, some senior Children's Department staff members have voiced doubts regarding the advisability and the feasibility of encouraging F.A.S. workers to engage in community and group work. One of the main objections was that the assigned officers do not have the specialised training essential for this type of service. Others maintain that Children's Departments have not been authorised to do this kind of work, and that there are agencies who specialise in this specific function. In some instances the feeling was conveyed to the Research Officer that there was a certain lack of awareness of the professional applications and the potentialities of the social work disciplines in relation to community organisation and group work.[1]

In a few departments the growing awareness of the problems posed by the existence of a densely populated high-need sector in the area has led to pioneering attempts at establishing Family Advice Centre 'outposts' which engage in community work in direct response to client needs, and with marked success. Here the worker became quickly convinced that the multiplicity of similar problems in certain areas of social and family life added up to common problems faced by the community. In fact, the major problem confronting the worker and his

---

[1] The following remark in a recent study of advice services may be of some interest here: 'The British have not developed the widespread local self-help and community action record characteristic of many American cities, partly because of the "Civil Rights" movement, and the anti-poverty war.' Alfred J. Kahn et al, *Neighbourhood Information Centres*, Columbia University School of Social Work, New York, 1966.

clients was the state of non-community which existed, for instance, in an estate populated by rehoused families from various slum-clearance areas of a large city. The department, in this particular case, regarded it as one of the worker's functions to help a group of isolated and problem-ridden families to become a community. Community-focused services provided by these F.A.S. outposts ranged from guiding a community in their efforts to have 'keep off the grass' signs removed so that their children could play on the lawn, instead of in the street, to a successful interceding on behalf of a specific population group with the local Housing Authority, which resulted in a reduction of rents which were unreasonably high in proportion to the average income of the people concerned.

The community work approach, which, to some degree, amounts to a shift of emphasis from the family *per se* to the family-within-the-community, has aroused much interest and discussion among the staff of the departments. Workers have commented that this approach may constitute a step forward towards the practical application of the F.A.S. functions of the earliest possible identification and prevention of social malfunction.

There have been some initial attempts in a few of the departments to utilise group experiences in the helping process, mainly in those F.A.S. units which have initiated auxiliary settings such as 'Mothers' Clubs', Play Groups, etc. These attempts seem, however, to have remained spontaneous and informal. In other words, while workers became aware of the benefits clients derived from the group experience, and responded to this insight by encouraging group activities and discussions, we found no instances of the systematic use of professional group work methods.[1]

---

[1] For the definition of 'professional group work' we refer to the following:

'The objectives of the group worker include provision for personal growth according to individual capacity and need, the adjustment of the individual to other persons, to groups and to society, and the motivation of the individual towards the improvement of society: the recognition by the individual of his own rights, abilities, and the differences of others...

'The group worker makes conscious use of his relation to the group, his knowledge of programme as a tool, and his understanding of the individual and of the group process, and recognises his responsibility both to individuals and groups with whom he works, and the larger social values he represents.' (Harleigh B. Trecker, ed. *Group Work Foundations and Frontiers*, Whiteside Inc., New York 1955, pp. 4, 5.)

Professor Konopka gives a broad definition: 'Social group work is a method of social work which helps individuals to enhance their social functioning through *purposeful* group experiences, and to cope more effectively with their personal, group or community problems.' (Gisela Konopka, *Social Group Work*, Prentice-Hall, Engelwood, N. J. 1963, p. 20.)

In the United States, graduate schools of social work teach group work as a social work specialisation.

A voluntary Young People's Advisory Service provided an interesting example of the difficulties encountered in recognising and meeting the need for such work.

A teenage girl contacted this service with an urgent request for advice because she feared that she was pregnant. Her fear proved to be unfounded, but a series of interviews with a qualified volunteer worker disclosed that this girl belonged to a group of a dozen or so adolescents, who congregated every night at a certain street corner and frequented a cafe of bad reputation. The girl told the worker that all her friends were engaged in sexually promiscuous and delinquent activities. She was asked to encourage her friends to seek the guidance of the advisory service. A number of girls subsequently contacted the service, and some of them showed up for one interview with the assigned worker. The situation strongly indicated the need for a group worker who would contact the girls at their meeting place, and use the group work process to help them 'work through' their problems, and to effect a change in their attitudes and behaviour.

No action was taken, perhaps mainly because the members of this voluntary service were not familiar with the concepts and uses of group work.

On several occasions staff members have expressed their interest in group work with regard to the Family Advice Service, and have stated that their practical experience indicates the need for group work services, especially in community settings, with mothers whose husbands are at work, with unwed mothers, and with teenagers of both sexes.

6. *Family Advice Service functions in relation to other agencies*

The functional relations of the Family Advice Service and other agencies can be categorised under three headings,
a. F.A.S. intake of referrals *from* other agencies;
b. F.A.S. referrals of clients *to* other agencies;
c. the co-ordinating role of the Family Advice Service.

a. *Referrals from other agencies*

It is generally accepted practice for Family Advice Services to serve clients referred by other statutory and voluntary agencies. In fact the intake of referrals is emphasised as a useful and necessary service to other agencies in the Children's Department's areas. In most departments the Family Advice Service was introduced with a concerted effort to convince other statutory and voluntary agencies in the area that an F.A.S. should be regarded as a willing and useful address to which to refer clients with a wide range of needs and problems.

The majority of the local agencies responded eagerly and referred clients in significant numbers. Only in one instance known to us was the intake of referrals *not* foreseen as one of the functions of the Family Advice Service. Here a report stated: 'It is not anticipated that other social agencies will refer people to the Advice Centre, its aim being primarily to help those who are not known to, or have fallen between, the social services available, and who need guidance in deciding who can give them the most positive support.'[1] Experience proved otherwise, and during the first six months of operation of this particular centre, clients were referred by Health Visitors, Mental Hygiene Clinics, Welfare Officers, the Housing Department, a number of voluntary agencies, as well as by the police, general practitioners, clergy, and the Town Hall.

In one of the Children's Departments we found some controversy regarding the intake of referrals. F.A.S. in this department consists of a unit within the Children's Department manned by rotating staff, and with functions which are not clearly distinguishable from those of other Child Care Officers. Staff members themselves say that they are willing and eager to accept referrals from other agencies, but a recently issued Survey by the Local Authority speaks of the Department's 'reputation for being reluctant to accept referrals'. [2]

The following listing of agencies who were found to refer clients to Family Advice Services in three different Children's Departments exemplifies the practice in almost all of the departments:[3]

Statutory agencies:

Health Visitors	Medical Social Workers
Housing Departments	National Assistance Board
Mental Welfare Officers	Probation Departments
Health Departments	School Welfare Officers
Dept. of Education	County and Borough Councillors
Police	Welfare Department
Transport Departments	Prison Welfare Services
Youth Employment Office	Children's Department
Disablement Resettlement Officers	

[1] Initial Report on the Family Advice Service by the Warden of Cambridge House in the London Borough of Southwark undated.
[2] What in fact happened was, that several Local Authority agencies referred a considerable number of multi-problem families which they themselves felt unable to serve, to the Children's Department, with a recommendation for long-term, intensive casework. The staff limitations and the overflowing current case-load of the Children's Department Family Casework Unit made the acceptance of these referrals impossible.
[3] This listing is not arranged in order of frequency or number of referrals.

Voluntary agencies:

Voluntary Legal Advice Centres	Voluntary Family Welfare Agencies
Marriage Guidance Counsellors	Moral Welfare
N.S.P.C.C.	Citizens' Advice Bureaux

A significant number of referrals were made by clergy, general practitioners, occupational therapists, solicitors, estate agents, and people classified as 'friends and neighbours'.

We did not obtain exact statistics, but are reasonably certain that the bulk of referrals comes from the following sources:

i. Health Visitors	ii. Housing Departments
iii. National Assistance Board	iv. General Practitioners

It should be pointed out that the incidence of referrals from one or another specific agency depends largely upon the degree to which Family Advice Services in the different departments have actively solicited such referrals, and upon the relationship Children's Department and F.A.S. staff have established with specific agencies.

The Department of Education steps in

The Divisional School Care Organiser contacted the Family Advice Service after a headmaster had become concerned about the physical neglect and irregular attendance of two teenage youngsters from the same family.

The Child Care Officer was assigned to investigate the case and visited the home of Mrs K, the mother of the two youngsters.

It was found that Mr and Mrs K, South Africans of European descent, had arrived from Africa three years ago to settle here. Some time after their arrival, Mr K returned to Africa, having obtained employment with the government of one of the newly independent countries. Mrs K remained behind with the two teenage children and one infant. Being a writer of some standing, Mrs K found employment in her field. The investigating Child Care Officer found her living in a fifteen-guinea a week flat under the most appalling conditions of filth and squalor.

Mrs K had completely lost control of her elder children, and appeared to be incapable of running the home and of adequately caring for her family. She seemed to have no insight into the difficulties experienced by the children, and to be unconcerned about the conditions under which they were living. Both the older children were of above average intelligence, but evidently emotionally disturbed.

The worker assigned to the case maintained contact with the school authorities in order to help the children make a better adjustment. The worker was also instrumental in having Mrs K and her oldest daughter undergo psychotherapy, which has resulted

in an improvement in their relationship. The youngest child had
to be received into the care of the Children's Department.

Mr K recently returned from Africa and his presence has brought
about some improvements in the family's living conditions.

The Children's Department is continuing casework with this
family at the present time.

While Family Advice Services have assigned considerable importance
to establishing themselves as widely used sources for referrals for other
agencies, there has been an increasing awareness of the significance of
'informal' referrals. This category comprises self-referrals (clients who
come on their own initiative, either because they have heard about the
service, or have seen it advertised, or have noticed the sign outside the
Children's Department or the detached Family Advice Centres) as well
as referrals by friends, neighbours and relatives. In almost all departments there has been a marked increase in the proportion of such
'informal' referrals, and this is generally regarded by staff as a measure
of success in establishing an image of the service as a 'safe, helpful and
easily accessible one'.[1]

In many cases, especially where the Family Advice Service operates
as an integrated unit of the Children's Department, and where F.A.S.
staff combine their F.A.S. functions with other duties, it is not always
clear whether the referrals made by other agencies are directed to the
Children's Department in general, or specifically to the Family Advice
Service. In some departments both cases occur, and it remains more or
less accidental whether a client is handled by the Family Advice
Service or other department. In one department the rule has been laid
down that all outside referrals are first to be submitted to the Children's
Officer, who assigns suitable cases to the F.A.S. worker. In those
departments where the identity of the Family Advice Service as a unit
with specific functions has been more clearly established, referrals are
made to the Family Advice Service by the Children's Department itself.

Last but not least it must be pointed out that many F.A.S. workers
feel that the mounting number of referrals by other agencies is, to some
degree, due to the fact that the 1963 Act has given Children's Departments the authority to offer financial assistance in all preventive and
rehabilitation cases which involve children. Staff members feel that those

---

[1] A remark made in a recent publication may be of some interest in this context. The
authors express the opinion that emphasis on achieving a preponderance of informal
referrals is directly related to the degree of success of creating an image of the Family
Advice Service which is 'the antithesis of the "snooper", "arbiter of public morals"
concept' (*A Family Service and a Family Court* by a Study Group of the Council for
Children's Welfare, London.)

referrals would have come to the Children's Department regardless of the existence of a Family Advice Service.

b. F.A.S. referrals to other agencies

It has proved somewhat more difficult to gain adequate impressions of the range and number of referrals to other statutory and voluntary agencies made by the Family Advice Services. This is largely due to the fact that 'simple advice' cases which are referred to the competent agency after brief interview have not been recorded in most of the departments. The Home Office Circular cited previously has advised staff that those cases disposed of 'by redirection to another department or agency should not be counted'.[1]

The impression was gained that F.A.S. staff has, in fact, referred clients to *all* statutory and voluntary agencies who were felt to be competent and willing to help any particular client with his specific problems. Frequency and incidence of F.A.S. referrals to any agency depended largely upon the degree of co-operation and the relationship existing between the Family Advice Service and other statutory or voluntary agencies, in any particular area.

The question whether referral is a function of an F.A.S., and what proportion of the worker's time and effort should be allotted to making the referrals, has become the subject for discussion in the field. Opinions differ widely. In some departments it is felt that referral to other agencies is, indeed, the main function of the Family Advice Service.[2] Here we found a tendency to assign the less trained and experienced workers to F.A.S. duties. In one department a clerical worker has been assigned who has the sole function of making referrals. In other departments referrals are regarded as incidental and secondary, while the worker's main function is seen as 'intensive casework'. Here executive staff hold that only trained, experienced workers with a high degree of diagnostic skill should be asked to fill F.A.S. positions. As a result of this latter view, one department has shelved the setting up of the Family Advice Service because of the present lack of suitable personnel.

Closely related to the above-mentioned problem, are two issues:

(i) The attitudes of professional practitioners to referral work, and
(ii) the conception of referrals as a social work skill.

Many trained caseworkers assigned to F.A.S. duties have voiced some

---

[1] Home Office Circular No. 96, 1 June 1966, Appendix C.
[2] One Report states: 'It was indicated that the Advice Centre would primarily be a sorting house, referring the majority of applicants to other agencies' (Initial Report on the Establishment of the Family Advice Service by the Warden of Cambridge House, London Borough of Southwark).

degree of resentment about having to allocate much of their time and effort to what they regard as work (referrals) which could be handled by persons less well qualified. A number of workers expressed their frustration over being put in a position in which they have to pass on cases which have aroused their interest and which present them with a certain professional challenge.

The impression was gained that the major difficulty in this area is to be sought in the worker's conception of referral as an unskilled clerical job. It appears that there is widespread lack of awareness of the fact that referral work is, on the contrary, a complex professional task which demands experience with a wide range of personality and socio-cultural traits, a high degree of diagnostic skill, and which involves an often complex process of enabling the client to accept his own need for a specific referral, the preparation of the client for this next step in the helping process and the guidance and support of the client in making constructive use of the service to which he is being referred.

Preparing for referral

Mrs J, an elderly lady, called at the F.A.S. office at the suggestion of her family doctor. She sought help for her stepson, a 40-year-old bachelor, who had been a good son and a steady worker until about six weeks before. Lately he had become unusually uncommunicative and worried. He ate irregularly, and finally walked out of his job without explanation. A few days ago he had stayed out all night, was picked up by the police, and charged with attempted larceny and carrying an offensive weapon. He appeared in court, but was unconditionally discharged.

The F.A.S. visited Mr J (the stepson) at home. It was obvious that he was troubled and disturbed, and he agreed readily to accept the worker's help in obtaining employment, and in being examined by a psychiatrist.

The F.A.S. worker spoke to Mr J's recent employer. The latter said that Mr J had been a good worker, but had, on occasions, behaved strangely, and although he himself was sympathetic he could not re-employ him. The worker accompanied Mr J to the Labour Exchange, where he registered, and then took him to the psychiatric out-patients' clinic of the mental hospital. Mr J was unable to sustain the tension of waiting, and walked out before anyone had seen him. The worker walked home with him, and obtained his promise to return to the hospital later that day. Mr J was not able to keep that promise.

A week later the F.A.S. worker visited Mr J again, and found him sitting in the hall. On this occasion Mrs J spoke to the worker, expressed great anxiety, and said that her stepson's presence in the house made her uneasy. The worker contacted the family's doctor, and with the latter's help, Mr J was persuaded to keep an appointment at the psychiatric clinic a few days later.

After seeing the psychiatrist, and while arrangements were being made to admit him to hospital for observation, he walked out again. The worker found him at home in a state of depression and anxiety. He could not be persuaded to enter hospital as a voluntary patient, and it was therefore arranged, again with the help of the family doctor, to have the Mental Health Department commit him to a mental hospital. Mr J was accompanied to the hospital by the F.A.S. worker.

Mrs J needed some support to deal with feelings of guilt regarding her stepson. In a series of talks, the F.A.S. worker was able to help her face the reality of the situation, and to allay her anxiety to some extent.

Mr J's condition was diagnosed as a state of severe paranoid delusion.

c. The Co-ordinating role of the Family Advice Service

The importance of inter-agency and inter-service co-ordination for effective F.A.S. work has been touched on in preceding sections of this study.

A Home Office Memorandum issued shortly after the publication of the 1963 Act states that in a number of areas steps have already been taken for 'improving co-ordination of local authority services', and for 'strengthening links with voluntary agencies'.[1]

The value of, and the need for, co-ordination of the wide range of social service agencies is so widely known and unanimously accepted that this need not be further expounded. Good and better co-ordination is, as every practitioner knows, 'something we can never get enough of'. At the same time almost every report dealing with any aspect of social services which has been written during the last decades is, at least mildly, critical of the widely felt lack of effective co-ordination. In part, this state of affairs has led to the, at times, somewhat too enthusiastic assignment of co-ordinating functions to many types of services. The enthusiasm is perhaps more justified in the case of the Family Advice Service, than in some other instances.

It has been held that an F.A.S. should initiate or improve co-ordination of the relevant agencies with the focus upon effective service to the client. This is summed up in a recent pamphlet which states that the Family Advice Service should seek to become 'a useful auxiliary and supporting service to... [other] agencies; it would in no sense compete with them'.[2]

[1] Home Office Memorandum on the Reports of Local Authorities, 1 October 1963 to 31 July 1964, p. 1.
[2] *A Family Service and a Family Court*, by a study group of the Council for Children's Welfare, London.

A Report by the Association of Children's Officers stated: 'The basic weakness in the present pattern is that there is no one body at national or at local level able to assume responsibility for the personal problems of a family as a whole, so that services are fragmented and sometimes do not follow a consistent pattern in dealing with the needs of particular families.'[1] In the Children's Departments visited it was hoped that the work of the Family Advice Service would be able to contribute importantly to the alleviation of this situation. It seems that this optimistic view was, at least partly, justified.

In almost all F.A.S. settings we visited, a more or less spontaneous 'grass-roots' co-ordination between F.A.S. staff and field staff of other statutory and voluntary agencies has taken place. This 'grass-roots' co-ordination is usually initiated by the F.A.S. worker, and based upon the concrete demands of the given situation, and geared to treatment goals. We found that, in a relatively short period of time, F.A.S. workers came into frequent contact with workers from other agencies in order to arrange referrals, exchange information, and/or discuss possible approaches to help a client. In most cases this leads to relationships of mutual respect and readiness for constructive co-operation between field staff of different agencies, as well as to an increased understanding of each other's methods, limitations, service traditions and frustrations. This kind of 'grass-roots' co-ordination tends to reduce red tape and appears to produce good practical results. It appeared that this type of co-ordination, which takes place on the field level, is often quite independent of policy decisions and implementations (such as co-ordinating committees) which are provided for at the inter-agency executive level.

In most departments top level co-ordinating committees had already functioned with varying degrees of effectiveness before the establishment of the Family Advice Services. This co-ordinating body usually consisted of the chief officers of all local statutory agencies and executive officers of the largest and most prestigious voluntary services. In many cases this committee is chaired by the Children's Officer. Many departments also convened periodic case conferences to which representatives of all the relevant statutory and voluntary agencies (and in some cases the clergy, general practitioners, solicitors, estate agents etc.) were invited. These case conferences aimed at co-ordinating services with regard to one or several particular client families. The 'grass-roots' co-ordination which functions informally, at short notice, and as the situation regarding the client demands, appears to be a relatively recent phenomenon, which

[1] *Evidence to the Committee on Local Authority and Allied Social Services by the Association of Children's Officers*, April 1966.

grew out of the broad and flexible functions of F.A.S. work and especially from its focus on prevention. Almost all F.A.S. staff we interviewed felt that the Family Advice Service was in a uniquely favourable position to foster and maintain this type of periodic co-ordination.

The staff of a Family Advice Service in a voluntary setting (a Settlement House) commented:

'Where a Family Advice Service is incorporated in an already existing agency, such as a Settlement House, offering Community Development and group work services, as well as some general social work, it is not the task of the Advice Service to extend its work into these fields. Where liaison meetings between local agency workers have already been established, the Advice Service does not initiate such meetings, but fulfils its own role within them. There is a greater emphasis on the casework skills of the F.A.S. worker, and in our own case we found that the worker comes close to functioning as a casework consultant to the Settlement's community workers. The special duties of the Advice Service lie in the area of knitting together the various social services provided for a family by a number of different agencies. The F.A.S. worker has also come to play an important part in dealing with inter-community tensions, and with conflict situations within and between different segments of the community.'

One F.A.S. worker established in a flat in a housing estate inhabited by a large number of multi-problem families, initiated periodic meetings of all the statutory and voluntary field workers who had clients within this particular block. At these meetings, individual clients and client families, as well as community problems, were discussed.

There are no limits set to the range of statutory and voluntary services whose workers are contacted by F.A.S. staff in order to co-ordinate activities. Existing undercurrents of inter-agency friction and workers' personalities do, of course, play an important role in determining the degree of co-operation that takes place. On the whole, however, quantity and quality of contacts between F.A.S. staff and field workers of other agencies were based upon the worker's diagnosis of clients' needs.

With some variations, 'grass-roots' co-ordination was established at various levels with the staff of *all* the local statutory and voluntary agencies, as well as with general practitioners, the clergy, solicitors and estate agents. Many departments report that there is especially close co-operation between F.A.S. staff and Health Visitors. Frequent co-operation is also reported with Housing Authorities' officials, Probation Officers, N.A.B. officials, general practitioners, the clergy and estate agents. F.A.S. workers appear to have been least successful in co-ordinating their work with that of Education Department staff. The reasons for this did not become apparent during this survey.

Physical proximity of F.A.S. facilities with the officers of other departments frequently appeared as of considerable benefit to better and more direct co-ordination. A detached Family Advice Centre located on the premises of the Probation Department in a small town, for instance, reported that they quickly established excellent relationships with the Probation Officers. Several F.A.S. workers who were given facilities in the offices of local Health Visitors state that this greatly advanced co-ordination of their work with that of these officials. As mentioned previously, the housing of four different statutory departments (Children's, Medical, Education, and Housing Departments) under the same roof in one of the boroughs of London, and the sharing of purpose-built facilities with a number of other statutory and voluntary locally assigned staff members from other agencies, greatly facilitated co-ordination between the agencies. On the other hand, we found that a local authority policy decision to integrate the services of the Children's Department and the Welfare Department by establishing a Family Advice Centre staffed by officers from both departments, failed to further the goal of co-ordination. The staff of this centre told us that the close working together tended to emphasise the 'very different methods and traditions' of the two departments.

The issue of the co-ordinating function of the Family Advice Service is also related to the well-known problem of the multiplicity of service to one client or client family. The Association of Child Care Officers stated:

'It could be debated whether better co-ordination could not result in one worker dealing with several aspects of the problems and reduce the confusion a little—but statutory duties allocated to particular workers, as well as departmental policies, make this impracticable. With the establishment of a Family Service, it could result in one worker giving the necessary support for the family, but this does not mean that in no circumstances should more than one social worker be involved with a family. The decision of the need for more than one worker to be involved should be based on the requirement of the family and its individual members, rather than on the organisation of the social services.'[1]

In most cases the better field level co-ordination initiated by F.A.S. staff seems in the main to have resulted in a better 'working together' towards the same goal, rather than in the reduction of workers involved

[1]A.C.C.O.'s *Evidence to Seebohm*, London, May 1966, p. 5.

with any particular case. In one department co-ordination committee case conferences introduced a policy of appointing a 'key worker' in cases where officers from several agencies dealt with the same client. (It is worth noting that in some instances a clergyman, general practitioner, or even a helpful lay member of the community was appointed.) We found that in many cases (whether by design or because his central function seemed to indicate this) the F.A.S. worker was appointed a 'key worker'.

5. Special Problems faced by the Family Advice Service

Our survey suggests that there are four problems which seem to have a significant bearing upon the development and operation of a Family Advice Service. These problems are:

1. Staffing.
2. Recording.
3. Duplication of Functions.
4. Conflict of Functions.

5·1 Staffing

The preceding discussion will have made it clear that, as in many other areas of Children's Department work, staffing constitutes a major problem for the operation of Family Advice Services. Many Children's Officers and Child Care Workers have stated that the lack of a sufficient number of trained staff acts as a brake on the work of existing Family Advice settings, limits the scope of operation of F.A.S. units, and curtails the setting up of additional Family Advice Centres. As already mentioned, one Children's Department has refrained from organising a Family Advice Service because of the lack of suitable personnel.

In addition to the widely expressed need for more social workers to man additional Family Advice Centres in specific high-need areas, many staff members state that the necessity for making part of their time available for regular Children's Department work seriously limits their capacity to meet the needs of the growing number of F.A.S. clients. The practice of assigning workers to both F.A.S. and other Children's Department duties, or to assign a great number of different workers in rotation to once-a-week or bi-weekly duty turns with the F.A.S. (a practice usually imposed by staff shortage), undoubtedly perpetuates and increases the difficulty of giving the F.A.S. an identity of its own;

it also reduced the likelihood of the worker establishing his specific role in the community.

Another aspect of the staffing problem is the, perhaps desirable, lack of demarcation lines between the different tasks and roles of the Children's Department field personnel. A statement by a senior staff member of the Liverpool Family Service Unit may be relevant here:

> 'It is becoming more difficult to differentiate between family casework, casework with people who are members of families, and casework in community care generally: this is an unmistakable sign of the trend towards a more family-centred approach throughout the social work services.'[1]

In many departments F.A.S. work has not been conceived as a new and distinct function, requiring a definite type of worker. This seems to have led to some degree of arbitrariness in the assignment of Child Care Officers, Family Caseworkers, and other persons of varying background, experience and qualifications to Family Advice Service duties.

In several well-established Family Advice Centres, the opinion has been expressed that more than one worker is needed to meet the demands of this service. Some people have suggested that F.A.S. units should include several kinds of workers to effect a certain division of labour. For instance, the idea has been put forward that an F.A.S. unit should consist of a receptionist (a clerical worker) who could also function as a filing clerk; a guidance worker, whose specific function would be short-term counselling (for which he should have the appropriate training, possibly including group work); and a caseworker who would offer intensive casework on a sustained basis, including home visits. This need for a team of workers seems especially urgent in those detached Family Advice Centres which have moved into high-need communities. Here the assignment of a community worker in addition to a field worker is thought to promise good results.

The difference of opinion between executive staff regarding the type of worker most suitable for F.A.S. work has already been touched on. It would seem that most Children's Officers and staff members feel that experienced, trained professionals are needed. It is our impression that practical experience of F.A.S. work appears to lend weight to this opinion. Several Children's Officers have stated emphatically that professionally trained, highly skilled social workers are needed in a setting in which much, perhaps all, depends upon the ability of the worker to establish rapport with the client during the initial interview.

[1] Sheila M. Kay, 'The Future Development of Family Casework in the Non-Statutory Social Services', *Social Casework*, July 1966, p. 10.

One Children's Officer[1] underlined this view with a quote from Helen H. Perlman (*So you want to be a Social Worker*, 1962):

'But now to turn to the person with a problem. As he crosses the threshold of the social agency, he may see it only as an office where "they" will or will not be able or willing to help him. This help, whether it is to enhance his physical, social, psychological welfare, or all three at once, is given by a process which combines professional methods and behaviour.'

A recent advertisement for an F.A.S. position in one of the Children's Departments states: 'A vigorous and imaginative worker is required who can couple casework skills with the ability to stimulate and guide local community initiative.'

A few departments have begun to turn their attention to the possibility of using volunteers to supplement Family Advice Service staff. So far this idea has not been put into practice. A number of workers seemed uneasy about the use of volunteers, and voiced strong reservations because of their lack of training and also the problem of confidentiality. A few Children's Department officials feel that carefully screened, specially qualified, volunteers would prove very helpful in carrying out such duties as receptionist work, interviewing, short-term counselling, and home visits, as well as providing auxiliary services, such as home help services, Mothers' Club work, and Play Group supervision. Here the stipulation was made that such volunteers be provided with constant professional consultation and supervision.

The Blackfriars Settlement, which introduced a Family Counselling project, financed by the Children's Department of the London Borough of Southwark under Section I of the 1963 Act, has stated that:

'...as long as they can be given adequate professional support, volunteers represent the most important element in its work, and should not be seen merely as auxiliaries. The Settlement believes the real fear, among some professional workers, that unskilled volunteers can do more harm than good, can be overcome by giving the Counsellors an increased awareness of the problems with which they are dealing, through their regular seminars and the personal supervision of the Caseworker.'[2]

This brings us to the problem of supervision, which is closely related, and perhaps basic, to the issue of adequate staffing.

[1] Mrs M. Decker, County Borough of Preston.
[2] 'Commentary', *Social Service Quarterly*, Autumn 1966, p. 47.

Only very few of the departments we visited were able to allocate enough time to ensure F.A.S. staff of adequate, consistent professional supervision. In most cases senior staff members are too busy with their own case loads, administrative duties, and the supervision of regular Child Care Officers and Family Caseworkers to be able to spare sufficient time at regular intervals for the supervision of F.A.S. staff. It also became apparent that in a number of departments there seemed to be a certain lack of awareness of any need for a regular system of professional supervision for F.A.S. staff. Several F.A.S. workers expressed some anxiety and frustration about this.

Individual workers stated that they were not sure of their roles and functions as Family Advice Service workers, that they felt 'isolated', 'set adrift to sink or swim', 'lost' or 'overwhelmed' by the great variety of problems with which clients confronted them.

In contrast to this, those workers who did receive adequate and consistent supervision by a specially assigned senior staff member emphasised the role of this professional support in their practical day to day work and expressed their feeling that their work in the Family Advice Service had become more rewarding and efficient because of the 'backing' provided by the department.

5·2 Recording

Systematic keeping of records and filing of case histories constitutes something of a problem in several of the F.A.S. units. Some departments maintain a well-organised and conscientious recording system, in which all essential data from each client (initial diagnostic summaries, continuous instalments of the case history, records of referrals, and follow-up reports) are kept up to date. In other departments the Family Advice Service has only a card index with some of the basic data, and reports of casework sessions are filed only sporadically. In several departments the records are not easily accessible to the F.A.S. worker because the material is filed with the bulk of records of the regular Children's Department's work.

Of course many F.A.S. workers are well aware of the value of disciplined record-keeping, and make good use of their files in maintaining a consistent level of treatment, as well as relying upon up to date records in their contact with other agencies on behalf of the client. However, some F.A.S. staff do not seem to assign sufficient importance to this part of their work, or do not receive adequate professional guidance in this area from supervisory staff; last but not least, many field workers are so overwhelmed by large case loads that they do not find time for recording.

Thus, in a number of cases, the seemingly harsh statement held true, that: 'Good record-keeping was still not sufficiently recognised as being a vital part of good social work – especially work with children.'[1]

5.3 Duplication of Functions

Concern over possible duplication of functions has been voiced in two ways:

a. Staff have mentioned duplication of F.A.S. duties and Children's Department work *per se*;
b. workers have expressed concern over apparent duplication of F.A.S. functions and the work of other agencies.

In one of the Children's Departments visited, the two last Annual Reports repeat that 'in certain instances it was difficult to differentiate between the normal advisory functions of the department and those of the (Family Advice) Centre'. This statement represents the feelings regarding possible duplication of functions in most of the areas which were visited.

In several departments it appears that F.A.S. workers and regular Child Care and/or Family Caseworkers (especially the latter) do almost exactly the same work, directed by the same goals and using the same methods and techniques. At times, the same individual staff member may be engaged in what the department regards as Family Advice Service work one or two days a week, while doing the same or a very similar job with other clients for the rest of the time. In some departments where this situation prevails, F.A.S. staff have additional specific functions (such as short-term counselling, co-ordinating work, supervision of clubs, etc.) which distinguishes their role to some degree from that of the regular staff. However, in some departments even this distinction is missing.

Several senior officers held that this situation has arisen because their departments have assigned workers to do what is, in fact, Family Advice Service work, long before this type of work was given a name and an identity of its own. In these cases the departments are now continuing a well-established practice under a new name in one corner of the department, while the rest of the department carries on with the same work as usual. In a few instances staff feel that the relatively recent assignment of Family Advice Work to a specific unit of the department may have been detrimental to the more desirable diffusion of the advice, guidance and assistance concepts throughout the department, and the

[1] A.C.C.O.'s *Evidence to Seebohm*, London, May 1966, p. 15.

wholehearted acceptance of this approach by all workers. Others, on the contrary, hold that the introduction of a specific name for this type of work, and its clear-cut delineation as a separate function, have put the Family Advice Service concept 'on the map' and increased the awareness of its value among the older staff of the department.

Duplication of function is least apparent in those departments where F.A.S. units have been 'contracted out' to Settlement Houses or Community Centres (F.A.S. staff in these settings regarding themselves mainly as voluntary agency workers), and those detached Family Advice Centres which have begun to focus upon community work.

Another area of concern and widespread discussion is the possible duplication of function of the Children's Department's Family Advice Service work with similar work done by other, mainly voluntary, agencies, such as the Family Service Unit, Advice Centres run by local councillors and, especially, the Citizens' Advice Bureaux. One Children's Department has shelved the setting up of its own Family Advice Service unit because the staff feels that a local Civic Information Bureau and the Social Care Committee, both set up under the auspices of the City Council, meet the needs of this type of service adequately.

It may serve to underline and spell out the possibility of duplication by providing for more detailed information on the services offered by those agencies who appear to do the same type of work as the Family Advice Service.[1]

The Social Care Committee mentioned above lists 389 enquiries in its statistical report for March 1966 under the following categories:

Accommodation (other than residential and temporary)	Furniture
	Clothing
Family problems	Accommodation in local housing estate
General welfare	General welfare of residents in Part 3
Legal advice	accommodation
Matrimonial problems	Medical services
Personal problems	Tenancy problems
Miscellaneous	

This agency employs trained staff and engages in casework, short-term counselling, and referrals (cases involving children in need of financial assistance are usually referred to the Children's Department). The offices are centrally located and easily accessible. The Social Care Committee's chief officer stressed the fact that no limits are set as to the

[1] The repeatedly expressed concern of Children's Department staff regarding the duplication of F.A.S. work by these agencies led the Research Officer to schedule a number of interviews with the staff of these services in the course of our enquiry.

type of client or the kind of problem dealt with. He stated: 'We never refer a case we can deal with ourselves.' This agency has a 24-hour telephone advisory service, an arrangement which does not exist in any of the F.A.S. settings that were seen.

The Civic Information Bureau mentioned above lists the following types of enquiries handled during the year 1965:

Old people's welfare	Cruelty to children
Matrimonial problems	Affiliation orders and problems
Non-contributory pensions	National Assistance
Change of name	Wills
Private insurance	Tax on unearned income
Post-war credits	Death and estate duties

While this agency employs no trained social workers, the officer in charge stated that a significant amount of long-term counselling, including home visits, is being done. The 1965 Report issued by this Bureau states: 'Although the more personal enquiries were comparatively few in number, the time which must be allotted to them was considerable: matrimonial cases where children were involved; unmarried mothers whose parents were unsympathetic; elderly persons whose families did not want the responsibility of their care – such cases made up a large proportion of this type of enquiry.'

Most concern has been aroused by Children's Departments' apparent duplication of functions arising from the work of the Citizens' Advice Bureaux, which have offices in almost all areas. For the following relevant details on the operations of the Citizens' Advice Bureaux we have made use of a recent study carried out by a team of American investigators,[1] as well as of our own enquiry.

C.A.B. states its purpose as follows: 'To make available to the individual accurate information and skilled advice on the many problems that arise in everyday life; to explain legislation; to help the citizen to benefit from and use wisely the services provided him by the State.'[2]

This statement leaves considerable leeway for doing the kind of advisory work which is regarded as a function of a Family Advice Service. Professor Kahn's impression of C.A.B. work indeed bears a marked resemblance to the activities of F.A.S. settings:

'Generally, the workers observed seemed to have all the time in the world, and much patience. They meet with some enquirers, again

[1] Alfred J. Kahn *et al.*, *Neighbourhood Information Centres*, Columbia University School of Social Work, New York, 1966.
[2] Cited in Kahn *et al.*, p. 16.

and again, occasionally visit homes, explore resources, and try to give the help needed. Although Bureaux encourage enquirers to help themselves, the workers also will take action on their behalf: write letters, fill out forms, do accounts, make appointments, telephone other agencies to explain the problem clearly.... Frequently, the true problem does not emerge immediately.... To the question of how far a worker should go with an enquirer, and when does C.A.B. work become casework, the answer depends on the availability of trained worker's services, and on the professional–volunteer balance of the particular Bureau's staff... for the most part, C.A.B.s lack the follow-up process.'[1]

Professor Kahn's study estimates that 60 per cent of C.A.B. cases concern 'straight information', while 40 per cent 'go beyond this'.[2]

The amount of casework done in Citizens' Advice Bureaux is mainly determined by the availability of trained staff in the different localities. The current study estimates that there is at present a ratio of 70 per cent to 30 per cent of untrained volunteers and trained social workers in C.A.B. employment.[3] There are some indications that the Citizens Advice Bureaux are making an effort to increase their trained staff.[4] In our more limited enquiry we found wide differences between the availability of trained workers, and therefore the amount of casework being offered, in C.A.B. settings. In one large city with one central and eight branch offices of the Citizens' Advice Bureau, approximately 80 volunteers and *no* trained social workers are employed. Here C.A.B. staff refers most cases needing help beyond simple information and advice to the relevant agencies.[5]

In another area in one of the London Boroughs a local Citizens' Advice Bureau is staffed exclusively by trained social workers and quite evidently duplicates the functions of the Family Advice Service in practically every aspect. Here the relations between C.A.B. and F.A.S. have a strongly competitive colouring. The Family Advice Service has attempted to alleviate this situation by emphasising the 'particular interest in families where there are young children'.

While in many of the departments we visited, the C.A.B. functions mainly as an information service and relations with the F.A.S.

1 Kahn *et al.*, pp. 18, 19.
2 Ibid., p. 20.
3 Ibid., p. 29.
4 See recent advertisements for 'Full-time social workers' specifying that 'applicants should have social work experience and preference is given to those with social work qualifications'.
5 From the Children's Officers' Report on the Co-ordination of Services working with Families at Risk.

constitute no problem, we found a significant number of cases in which Children's Department and F.A.S. staff expressed their uneasiness about an apparent duplication of services by the two agencies; and it was felt that this matter ought to be cleared up by policy decisions as soon as possible.

One County Children's Department Area Officer suggested a solution by offering Children's Department participation in the financing of a Citizens' Advice Bureau in which the Children's Department F.A.S. worker would be given office space on the premises, and work in close co-operation with the non-professional C.A.B. staff.

5.4 Conflict of Functions

Apparent or anticipated conflict between statutory obligations and the advice, guidance and assistance functions of the Family Advice Service have been a subject for discussion in the field. Specifically, workers are concerned with the possible incompatibility of their statutory obligations under Section 2 of the Children and Young Persons Act, 1952 and the F.A.S. goal of creating the image of a 'safe', 'easily accessible, confidential, no-strings-attached', service, geared to inducing the widest possible range of clients to seek help and advice with their problems at a pre-crisis stage. This apprehension is based on the assumption that certain, especially unskilled, semiskilled, and now immigrant, population groups regard the statutory services as powerful, threatening, authority-wielding bodies, and are likely to react to them with fear, distrust, or even open hostility.

This assumption seems to have found some support in practical experience. A number of workers feel that many clients who would benefit from the service keep away because they identify the F.A.S. worker as a Child Care Officer, and are afraid to 'get into trouble'. In two instances C.A.B. officials reported that their attempts to refer lower-class clients to the Family Advice Service of the Children's Department frequently met with the reply: 'We came to you, because we don't want to go there. Those are the people who take your children away.'[1]

[1] The personal experience of the writer of this Report in 'detached' or 'street club' work in the United States and Israel offers some interesting parallels:

In street club work a trained group worker establishes a relationship of mutual confidence and acceptance with a 'gang' or 'street-corner group' of delinquent teenagers in their own environment, in effect at their usual 'hang-out'. In order to succeed in his efforts to bring about fundamental changes in the norms and in the behaviour of the group, the worker must establish his image as a person who can be trusted implicitly, a knowledgeable resourceful adult whom 'you can tell everything'. In the course of his work, this type of social worker obtains knowledge of a wide range of unlawful activities. As a citizen he is obliged to convey all information regarding criminal acts to the law enforcement agencies. Failure to do so may implicate him as an accessory to crime. As

An offence has been committed

The local newspaper on the Children's Officer's desk that morning carried a fat headline on the front page: 'New Born Infant Abandoned in Church – Police Investigating.'

An hour later the baby had arrived at the Children's Department in the arms of a police matron and arrangements were immediately made for temporary foster care.

For a week this case was the sensation of the small town, then other topics took their place in the newspapers.

One afternoon, about three weeks later, a nervous young man, barely out of his teens, came into the F.A.S. office. He wanted to know whether it was all right for him to talk about something that happened to a friend. 'Mind you, it isn't anything that I'm involved in. A friend of mine didn't want to come, so I'm just trying to help. It's got nothing to do with me.'

With a few reassuring words the worker put the young man at his ease, and he asked his question:

'What happens if a girl, a young girl, has a baby without being married, and then gets all upset and puts the baby out for someone to find? If she wants to come and talk to you, maybe because she changed her mind and wants the baby back, feeling that she's done something wrong, is she going to be taken to the police?'

The F.A.S. worker took a deep breath, then answered calmly and honestly. She explained that abandoning a child is an offence against the law, and that, while the Family Advice Service, as part of the Children's Department, would do everything possible to help and to ensure the welfare of the child as well as the mother, the authorities would have to be informed. The worker assured the anxious young client that the local police shared his concern for the wellbeing of mother and child and could be relied upon to show sympathy and understanding. She asked the young man to do all he could to persuade the young woman in question to come to the Family Advice Service and talk to her. She told him that, as a friend, this was the best advice he could give the girl and asked him to tell her that the baby was well taken care of.

The following day a frightened 15-year-old girl sat down across the desk from the F.A.S. worker. She told her that she was the mother of the infant who had been found in the church a little over three weeks ago. She was full of feelings of guilt and remorse, and

---

a professional, the worker knows that his task of rehabilitating a group of delinquents has met with failure and become futile the very moment the youngsters learn that he has passed on to the authorities information they have given him. In the writer's experience in the field, as well as director of a street club project, it was always possible to obtain the understanding and co-operation of the police and the courts in this predicament. In the United States, as well as in Israel, the police and the courts readily accepted the street club workers' explanations and freed them from any obligation to divulge information obtained in the course of their work. The only exceptions were capital crimes, such as murder, which, luckily, occur very rarely.

wanted to do 'what's right', but implored the worker not to tell her parents and not to call the police.

As kindly and gently as possible, the worker made Susan face the realities of the situation. First of all she would have to tell her parents what happened. No matter how hurt and angry her parents might be, the matter could not be kept a secret for ever and it would be much worse if they found out themselves. The worker offered to come with the girl when she confronted her parents, and to lend her her support.

As a next step the official side would have to be straightened out. The worker explained that, under the law, she was obliged to inform the police, who had opened a file on the case, and had been looking for the mother of the abandoned child ever since the infant was found. Susan would have to face the fact that she had broken the law and that she owed the authorities an explanation. No, she would not have to go to jail, but the consequences, no matter how unpleasant, would have to be faced.

There remained the question of the father. The police would want to know the name of the boy and would insist on talking to him. Again, this was the law, and, after all, the young man must be expected to stand by Susan's side and help her to get through the difficult days ahead.

Susan and the worker talked for over an hour. Then, after her second cup of tea, Susan made her decision. She said that she would tell her parents. She would do it alone and would ask her parents to come to the F.A.S. office to talk to the worker. She would then accompany the worker to the Police Station to be interviewed. She gave the father's name and said that she would try to bring him with them.

During the next few days the worker met the young man, a frightened and confused 18-year-old boy. She had a long talk with Susan's parents and with the parents of the boy, helping them over their first shock and anger, and enabling them to adopt an understanding and supportive, rather than a punitive, attitude.

The police acted humanely, motivated solely by the wish to impress upon both young people the wrongness of their behaviour and to ensure that no irreparable damage to either of the youngsters should result from the situation. Both were firmly and strongly cautioned, and released to their homes.

In agreement with the two young people and their parents, adoption in a suitable home was arranged for the baby. Susan, the young man and the parents of both, remained in contact with the worker, and came to the office several times to talk about their feelings and to ask for further guidance.

From the first moment of the Children's Department's involvement in this case, strict confidentiality was maintained. The police co-operated fully and damaging publicity was avoided. In fact, the local press did not report the news of the identification of the abandoned infant's parents and the names of the two families involved were not disclosed to the public.

Some time later the F.A.S. worker found occasion to thank the young man who had initially contacted her and persuaded Susan to come to the office. She told him that he had acted as a true friend.

A voluntary agency which established a Children's Department financed Family Advice Centre on its premises reported: 'It was agreed that although money was provided by the Children's Department, the case-worker herself should be a member of the Settlement staff rather than the department; this is in order not to deceive the public by concealing the brawny arm of authority under the soft sleeves of [the Settlement House], and in order to achieve genuine confidentiality.' The same concern over possible conflict with regard to statutory and F.A.S. functions is expressed in the following passage:

'The Family Advice Centres must act and be seen to act entirely in the interests of those who come to them for help. They must never become yet another agency which can be identified with "the authorities" or with "them" in the "us and them" controversy.'[1]

A number of workers maintain that their own conflicting feelings about their statutory obligations and their F.A.S. role affects their practice and leaves them in somewhat of a quandary in cases where a client is reluctant to discuss his children, and insists upon limiting his request for help to the presented problem. One area Officer states categorically that the F.A.S. worker's statutory duties must be given precedence over all other considerations in the performance of his tasks. Several staff members maintain that the Children's Department in their area has established a sufficiently benevolent and permissive image in the community, so that no one is scared away by their statutory functions.[2]

---

[1] *A Family Service and a Family Court* by a Study Group of the Council for Children's Welfare (the implication that statutory agencies 'do not or are not conceived to act entirely in the interests of those who come to them for help' should be noted).
[2] The following incident experienced by the Research Officer may throw some doubt upon this view. Stopping at a pub in the late afternoon to have a glass of beer with two senior staff members who had indicated the above view, our entrance aroused the concern of a lady with two young children sitting at one of the tables. Obviously flustered, she greeted the Child Care Officers and asked jokingly: 'You are not going to report me, are you?' adding 'We only came in for a sandwich.' The officers replied jocularly and in a friendly manner. It was, however, obvious that the woman was aware of the officers' authority, and anxious because of her mild infraction of the rules.

'I want a simple answer to a simple question'

A few minutes before closing-time a man dressed in work overalls came into the Family Advice Service office. 'I'm in a bit of a rush,' he said, 'I only wanted to ask a question: they turned off my electricity because I didn't pay a few bills. Now I want to get it turned on again and pay it off at a £1 or so a month. The chap at the Electricity Board won't listen to anything. Can you tell me what can be done?'

The worker persuaded the man to sit down, in order to discuss the matter, but, after weighing several possibilities, had to admit that it might prove very difficult to persuade the Electricity Board to agree to this arrangement.

Mr Jones, the man with the problem, urged the F.A.S. worker: 'You've got to help me. I can't go on living by candle light. It's ruining my family. A man gets into trouble and he tries to get out of it, but I can't put down £17 all at once. I have two kids, you see. My daughter is fourteen, and since we have no light at home she's started to stay out late. I'm sure she's getting into trouble. I've given her a beating, but what's the use, what can she do at home, with no light and no telly? My son is twelve. He used to do well at school, but now his teacher has written a note saying that he wasn't doing his homework and somebody from school came round to say that he's been truanting several times. My wife is in a temper too. I just have to have that light turned on.'

The F.A.S. worker suggested to Mr Jones that he return the next morning, and she would contact the Welfare Department to see if they could help in this matter. But the worker became concerned with the problems this situation seemed to have caused Mr Jones's children. She asked Mr Jones to give her some more information regarding his son and his daughter, offering to visit the home and have a talk with both of them. Mr Jones was visibly annoyed. 'Never mind that,' he said, 'all I want you to do is help me pay off my electric bill and get the lights turned on. I'll look after the kids.'

The worker was gently insistent and explained that, after all, he had come to the Children's Department and the welfare of children was her concern. When Mr Jones persisted in his refusal to discuss his children's difficulties, the F.A.S. worker told him somewhat more bluntly that while she was quite willing to do all in her power to help Mr Jones to straighten out his relationship with the Electricity Board, it was her statutory duty to concern herself with the welfare of the 14-year-old girl who stayed out at night without the permission of her parents, and with the truancy of the 12-year-old boy.

Mr Jones seemed somewhat subdued, but could not hide his resentment. 'I daresay I talk too much,' he said, 'I thought you were going to tell me how I could straighten out my electric bill. All I want is a simple answer to a simple question, and look where it has got me. Now I'm in trouble about my children.'

Smiling, the worker tried to soothe Mr Jones's ruffled feelings.

'You're not in any trouble,' she assured him, 'I am only trying to help and fully understand your difficulties.'

Mr Jones promised to return the next morning, but he did not leave his address and he did not come back.

Apart from the obvious area of potential conflict between statutory and F.A.S. functions, which pertains directly to children 'at risk', another source of potential conflict was brought to our attention by Children's Department staff: Under the Matrimonial Proceedings (Children) Act, 1958 and the Matrimonial Proceedings (Magistrate's Court) Act, 1960 the Children's Department may be obliged by the Court to give evidence or provide information concerning the custody of children in divorce or matrimonial dispute cases. Matrimonial problems involving children constitute a sizeable proportion of the case loads of F.A.S. units we have visited. There seems to be a very real possibility, therefore, that the F.A.S. worker may be put in a position of having to make statutory use of information he has acquired in the confidential, 'no-strings-attached' setting of the Family Advice Service.[1]

Those few workers who have been assigned to detached Family Advice Centres serving specific high-need communities, appear to be least affected by this role conflict problem. Their success in establishing their image as community workers, and in forming close and trusting relationships with their client groups, tends to make the question of their official function irrelevant.

The issue of possible conflict between statutory and F.A.S. functions has led a number of practitioners to question whether the Family Advice Service should operate under the auspices of Children's Departments. The placement of Family Advice Centres in local voluntary agencies (Settlement Houses or Community Centres) seems to provide one possible alternative solution. One report stated:

'There is little doubt that the general public would more readily turn to an Advice Centre with no apparent affiliations, and it would hope, in particular, that this would encourage young people to come...the worker would also benefit from working within a voluntary setting, because being part of an independent unit gave her greater scope for elasticity and quick change of plans; by calling her a social worker rather than a Child Care Officer, it was hoped that the appeal of the Centre would be broader, and would encourage people to come

[1] It must be pointed out that in practice, actual cases of the conflict-of-functions type described here occur only rarely. Nevertheless, the possibility of their occurrence has become the object of some concern.

whatever their problems were. The transfer of the project to an independent setting reduced the possibility of unfavourable inter-action with other functions of the Children's Department, and the possibility of clients being confused.'[1]

A Children's Officer pointed out that the Ingleby Committee 'recommended new powers in providing advice, guidance and assistance to families at risk, but did not feel able to suggest which department of Local Government should have these new powers'.[2] Some practitioners feel that this issue has not yet been satisfactorily resolved.

A recently issued Home Office memorandum suggests that Children's Departments may, under certain circumstances, establish F.A.S. units in conjunction with the Citizens' Advice Bureaux.[3] Several senior staff members in the Children's Department have suggested going one step further by considering delegating the F.A.S. function to the Citizens' Advice Bureaux.

In all departments we found much speculation regarding the place of the Family Advice Service in the projected unified Family Service, which is expected to result from the findings of the Seebohm Committee. It was felt that any effective planning for the future role of F.A.S. within a unified social service system will have to give consideration to the question of possible conflict between statutory and F.A.S. functions.

[1] Initial Report on the Family Advice Service by the Warden of Cambridge House' London Borough of Southwark, undated.
[2] Barbara J. Kahan, 'The Child, The Family and the Young Offender', *The British Journal of Criminology*, April 1966, p. 164.
[3] Factual Memorandum by the Home Office on the Local Authority Children's Service in England and Wales, February 1966, Appendix D.

6. Planning for the Future

Most Children's Departments are at present discussing future plans for the improvement of existing Family Advice Services and for the setting up of F.A.S. facilities where none exist.

In several departments plans are under way to supplement present F.A.S. staff, to increase the reception hours (in some cases evening and weekend services are being considered), and to effect more efficient allocation of functions within the F.A.S. units, for instance by staffing the unit with a receptionist, a worker who receives clients in the office and provides short-term counselling, and an additional worker who takes on intensive casework, including home visits.

Several departments are planning to set up a number of additional Family Advice Service 'outposts' in 'high need' areas or for population groups for whom the central office is not easily accessible. Most of these 'detached' Family Advice Centres are intended to be located on the premises of other local agencies such as the Probation Department, Infant Care Clinics, Welfare Departments, etc.; several are planned in local Settlement Houses or Community Centres. In a few instances it is planned to incorporate a Family Advice Centre in a purpose-built social service or family care centre.

An especially attractive plan is under consideration in a voluntary neighbourhood association which is constructing a 'Family Centre' on the outskirts of a large city in an area which houses a majority of Indian and African immigrants.

'The Family Centre will work towards a fuller and happier life for all who live in Sparkbrook. The Family Centre will provide: a Family Advice Centre; a Nursery Play Centre; a hall for the use of clubs; group activities, and social occasions. Interviewing rooms and offices for social workers doing preventive casework with families. Rooms for the use of voluntary and statutory bodies. An office for the Organiser,

71

who will be responsible for co-ordinating and extending the work of the Centre, and linking it with the activities of the Sparkbrook Association, and Statutory and Voluntary services. A Common Room, with library and canteen, to serve as a meeting ground for workers in these services.'[1]

The Children's Department of this area has shown active interest in providing some of the staff for this projected Family Advice Centre.

In one rural area the Children's Officer has suggested that Family Advice Services be provided for the population of a considerable number of small, geographically isolated, villages by organising a mobile F.A.S. post in a caravan on the model of travelling libraries which operate in these areas. Many departments have shown great interest in experimenting with community-based Family Advice out-posts with a community work focus. This holds good especially for those areas in which substantial pockets of 'unreached' problem families have been identified.

Understandably, much of the thinking and planning with regard to the further development of the Family Advice Service has been affected by the general anticipation of the findings of the Seebohm Committee. In some cases this seems to have had a negative effect in that it has induced executive personnel to recommend postponement of needed changes and future planning until the Committee's recommendations are published. In many departments, however, discussions about the role of F.A.S. in a unified social service are taking place. Many prac-titioners have reacted with considerable interest to the discussion of this subject in recent articles, as illustrated by the two following excerpts:

'The main aspect of the Family Service of which the public would be conscious would be the local Family Advice Centre...we see this development by the Family Service as a crucial piece of preventive work. These Centres would be the shop window of the service and would emphasise the availability of the service to the whole com-munity and not its exclusive concentration on the minority of citizens with long-term and intractable problems.'[2]

'The establishment of Centres where help can be given to all who need it, is welcomed by the [Child Care Officers] Association. It would be a pity if these Family Advice Centres should simply be used as a means of administering the Service. They should be placed in easily accessible points in centres of population. They should be well

---

[1] From a pamphlet issued by the Sparkbrook, Birmingham, Neighbourhood Association.
[2] *A Family Service and a Family Court*, cited above, p. 10.

designed, and attractively furnished, in buildings appropriate to the locality, and acceptable to the people it is hoped to serve. It is important that the Centres should be well known in the neighbourhood, so that they could be used as points of referral by teachers, doctors, clergymen, and the public generally. However, they are likely to be used as a base from which a team of social workers serves a neighbourhood.'[1]

In concluding this chapter, it may be added that we found, in discussing the future scope of the Family Advice Service, that many practitioners are especially concerned that two aspects be included at the planning stage:

a. The consideration of a possible need for specialised training for a new type of Family Advice Service Counsellor. This type of worker would receive training which differs somewhat from the conventional casework curriculum. Some emphasis on interviewing techniques, the referral process, wide knowledge of the functioning of other statutory and voluntary services, and courses on the implications of different socio-cultural milieux upon social work practice, are indicated.[2]

Margot Jefferys wrote:

'All social workers should be knowledgeable about the social and economic circumstances in which people live. They must appreciate the influence of kin, neighbourhood, school, religion, the work unit, the other formal and informal groups in the formation and maintenance of community and group norms and values, and in the attitudes displayed towards those who deviate from these norms.[3]

It has become apparent to many practitioners concerned with the future of the Family Advice Service that this particular social work setting has lent new urgency to the need for the training described above. At the same time, F.A.S. experience seems to offer unique opportunities for acquiring a broad range of down to earth, factual, knowledge about the economic, socio-cultural and psychological factors which impinge upon the lives of individuals, families, groups and communities. In some instances workers with F.A.S. experience seem to feel that plans for the future training of F.A.S. staff should consider putting greater emphasis

[1] A.C.C.O.'s *Evidence to Seebohm*, cited above, p. 21.
[2] Dr Gordon Rose of the Department of Social Administration at Manchester University, who himself directs an experimental community organisation project, has, in conversation with our Research Officer, expressed his concern over the lack of socio-cultural information provided by the conventional social studies curricula.
[3] *Anatomy of Social Welfare Services*, London, 1965, p. 306.

upon clinical skills and psychogeneric concepts (mainly based upon psychoanalytic theory).[1]

b. Several staff members feel that, as part of its co-ordinating functions, the Family Advice Service should initiate the setting up of 'Central Registers' into which the relevant statutory and voluntary agencies would feed essential data on the services provided to clients and client families. There is thought to be a marked need for such a system which would constitute a short cut in gathering the necessary information about the client, and would serve to prevent overlapping, duplication, and inconsistencies of services.

A number of practitioners are giving considerable thought to the question as to whether the Family Advice Service should continue to be regarded as part of the statutory function of the Children's Departments, or whether more attention should be paid to the potentialities of voluntary settings in the future planning of the service.

One Children's Officer stated:

'If the Family Advice Service becomes statutory, there is not only an obligation to supply the service, but it is open to public criticism if this is not done in a manner to suit the public. It therefore has to be rather more efficient and comprehensive than if done by a voluntary body.'[2]

[1] This points up an interesting difference between this country and the recent developments in the United States. American social work has, for some time, been predominantly under the influence of psychoanalytic theory, and has tended to neglect the practical, down to earth, helping approach which is taken for granted in British social work. In recent years, partly under the impact of the Civil Rights Movement and the 'War on Poverty' programmes, many leading American practitioners and social agencies have begun to question the relevance and effectiveness of this clinical orientation especially with regard to lower class clients. There has been a marked shift away from clinical methods, towards greater emphasis upon 'grass-roots', practical helping services, pioneered by group and community organisation workers. In fact, New York's 'Mobilisation for Youth' and other similar projects, have introduced the type of easily accessible, 'advice, guidance and assistance' services under such headings as 'Store-Front' casework, which the English Family Advice Service represents. These types of services are recommended, precisely, because they de-emphasise the clinical approach, and thereby seem to be more effective in meeting the needs of lower class populations, more especially the hard-to-reach groups and communities

[2] *Written communication from Mrs M. B. Armitage, Deputy Children's Officer, City of Sheffield Children's Department.*

7. Indications for Research

In all departments which were visited, staff on all levels expressed the need for research relevant to Family Advice Service practice. It was also found that almost everyone was well aware of the omission of preliminary research and consequent gaps in essential information and conceptualisation. There appears to be a consensus of opinion that, to ensure that Family Advice Services become effective and efficient, more needs to be known in three major areas:

a. the quantity, kind, and distribution of client needs for Family Advice Services;
b. content and methods of the services which the various types of F.A.S. settings offer at present;
c. immediate and long-range effects of F.A.S. work, and client reactions to the service.

In addition, staff members expressed a lively interest in receiving as much information as possible regarding the work of other statutory and voluntary agencies who are setting up advice services.

Many practitioners, especially among senior staff, stated that there was a need for 'ongoing' research, to provide a continuous source of information and knowledge for the practitioner, thereby contributing decisively to the correction of past mistakes and to the planning of future improvements in the service. The statement of the 1964 Children's Officers' Conference applies here: 'What may be described as "operational" research can then be employed to clarify objectives, track down difficulties, and modify the system to render it more effective.'[1]

In all departments, senior staff expressed their frustration regarding the fact that lack of time and personnel had hitherto prevented adequate research investigations. Many Children's Officers felt that the inclusion

[1] *Proceedings of the Fifteenth Annual Conference of the Association of Children's Officers*, Oxford, 1964, p. 43.

of a permanent post of Research Officer in the establishment of the departments would be highly desirable.

In some instances brief exploratory surveys have been carried out, and were found to have been of great benefit to subsequent F.A.S. work, although these surveys did not carry the authority of systematic studies.

In several departments some time was spent on gathering impressions on client needs and on the distribution of problem families in the area. Usually there was some consultation with field staff of other agencies, especially Health Visitors.

In one area the four statutory agencies (Health, Housing, Welfare, and Children's Departments) who jointly operate an F.A.S. unit, have commissioned the Social Research Unit of a local university to undertake a detailed study of the extent and character of the social and medical needs of the borough's population for the coming ten years, and of '...ways of deploying available manpower and material resources to meet such predicted needs'.[1]

In one London borough the worker who was charged with the task of setting up an F.A.S. outpost in a high-need community was given a period of three months to enquire into the living conditions and the socio-cultural milieu of this particular community, prior to the opening of the Centre.

In another department 'household statistics' are being compiled continuously, in order to make available this material for an evaluation of the uses clients make of the service.

No case has been found of a department attempting to gather information on client reactions to the service, or to devise means of determining the 'image' which the Family Advice Service has acquired among the various social groups and communities.

Arising from this exploratory investigation there are a number of indications for fuller research, such as the following:

1. There is a need to identify those types of services offered by other agencies (for instance C.A.B., F.S.U., F.W.A., Health Department Advice Centres, City or County Councillors' Advice Services, etc.) which seem to duplicate the Family Advice Service. A brief, systematic study of these services could provide this information.

2. There is a need to find out which population strata and what type of communities show the highest incidence of need for Family Advice Services.

[1] From a proposal submitted in January 1966.

Here information would have to be obtained on the type, quantity, and accessibility of existing social services which serve different population groups. Social strata would have to be categorised for this purpose.[1] It would also be necessary to distinguish different socio-cultural groups (immigrant, and different ethnic groups) and to differentiate between distinct types of communities (middle-class, working-class and lower-class communities, slum neighbourhoods, concentrations of re-housed slum dwellers, temporary migrant workers, etc.).

3. There is a need to establish what use different types of clients make of existing Family Advice Services, what problems they present, how they present their problems, what type of help they request (which may differ significantly from the kind of help they actually need) what kind of relationships they establish with F.A.S. staff. This would demand, methodologically speaking, close observation of the operation of several different types of F.A.S. settings, combined with the analysis of systematic, and conscientiously compiled, records for a period of at least one year.

4. Client reactions to the type of service provided by F.A.S. demand closer scrutiny. This can be regarded as an extension of the question: How do different types of clients use the service? However, here the focus would have to be upon the practical effects of F.A.S. work, to find out:

a. whether any given case of advice, guidance, or assistance elicits the intended response from the client, or else causes unpredicted or secondary reactions;

b. what, in concrete fact, are clients' reactions to specific instances of the helping service.

Methodology here would probably include the selection of sample groups of different categories of clients, the use of questionnaires and the analysis of F.A.S. reports.

5. Obviously, practitioners want to know whether people have indeed been helped by the Family Advice Service, what changes have been effected, and how the helping process has brought these changes about.

This type of study would include the use of questionnaires, and the interviewing of clients, as well as an analysis of case histories. One or several follow-up studies may be indicated.

[1] The Hounslow Project survey, for instance, made the following distinctions: (1) professional, managerial and business; (2) lesser professions, lower managerial and highly skilled; (3) skilled and semi-skilled; (4) unskilled, manual; (5) old-age pensioners, unemployed, and those earning less than £7 10s 0d per week. (E. Heimler *Experiments in Community Care, The Hounslow Project,* July 1966.)

6. There is a definite need for facts and figures on the degree and amount of interaction between F.A.S. units and other agencies. Statistical material would be analysed on such questions as referrals *by* other agencies, F.A.S. referrals *to* other agencies, and the incidence of contacts, meetings, and conferences between F.A.S. staff and the officials of other services. This material would have to be collected for a period of at least a year.

The areas of research listed above appeared indicated by the expressed needs and concerns of field workers and senior staff of the departments which participated in this exploratory study. Either separate investigations could be undertaken or else one comprehensive long-term study of several, and different, types of F.A.S., could be mounted.

It would be especially interesting and useful to focus one such comprehensive study upon the operation of a Family Advice 'outpost', set up within a high-need community. Methodologically, this kind of study would best be carried out through participant observation, resulting in a descriptive report on the social milieu of the community, the day-by-day operation of the service, and the effects of the Family Advice Service upon the community itself, as well as upon individual clients and client families. This type of study is well suited to trying out experimental approaches, such as those carried out by the Hounslow Project, which has recommended:

...a group approach to explore in greater depth the areas of possible primary prevention....Groups of 6–8 people are being brought together, who, in the ordinary course of their lives, are exposed to change and crises. Such groups will comprise school leavers, expectant mothers, young parents, the unemployed, the bereaved, the retired, the aged, etc.'[1]

In conclusion, this study confirmed the need for the kind of 'applied research...designed to help the practitioners' recommended by the 1964 Conference of the Association of Children's Officers.[2]

'Some of it may be called "exploratory"; it describes and clarifies a situation, focusing our attention on salient, interesting, or contradictory features of the situation; and it may enable its authors or readers to propose further developments in policy and practice.'[3]

[1] E. Heimler, *Experiments in Community Care, The Hounslow Project*, July 1966.
[2] *Proceedings of the Fifteenth Annual Conference of the Association of Children's Officers*, Oxford 1964, p. 42.
[3] Ibid., p. 42.

8. Concluding Remarks

In this section are summarised the most salient, though tentative, findings, which have been discussed in the body of this Report.

1. In all the Children's Departments which were visited a positive attitude was found towards the basic concepts underlying the Family Advice Service approach. These concepts, namely that the family should be regarded as the basic client unit, and that the focus should be upon early prevention,[1] appear to have had a decisive influence upon the overall service of the departments; indeed they appear to have guided their work to varying extents for some years prior to the publication of the 1963 Children and Young Persons Act.

The 1963 Act, and the subsequent recommendation for the establishment of Family Advice Services, gave the family-focused, preventive approach new impetus; it also drew attention to the preventive potentialities of easily accessible and broadly conceived advice, guidance and assistance services.

2. Family Advice Services have been established in most of the departments in four distinct forms:

(i) As internal parts of the Children's Department central or area offices.

(ii) As units serving several local and/or statutory agencies.

(iii) Under the auspices of a voluntary agency, financed and partly supervised by the Children's Department.

(iv) As detached centres or 'outposts' serving a specific sub-area, neighbourhood or community.

---

[1] The term 'early prevention' as it is generally understood by practitioners, and as we use it in this study, includes the 'primary' and 'secondary' stages of prevention as defined by Dr Kellmer Pringle in the chapter 'The Challenge of Prevention', in *Investment in Children*, ed. M. L. Kellmer Pringle, Longmans, London, 1965, pp. 133–42. We distinguish 'early prevention' from 'rehabilitation' or 'tertiary prevention' (ibid., pp. 142–50).

We found those F.A.S. 'outposts' which were established in high-need communities especially interesting and rich in potentialities. These types of F.A.S. settings showed a marked tendency to regard the community as the basic client unit, and to allot much time and effort to community work.[1]

3. In those few Children's Departments where an F.A.S. is not operating as a distinct service, the reason is not to be sought in a rejection of the underlying concepts, or in a denial of the need for this service, but rather in a number of special circumstances and limitations which appeared to make the setting up of F.A.S. units technically impossible or superfluous.[2]

4. The impression was gained that the traditional 'grass-roots' practical assistance and support approach of British social work, which is still dominant in the Children's Departments we visited, is eminently suitable for carrying out the functions, and achieving the goals, of the Family Advice Service. There are, on the other hand, indications that a shift to greater emphasis on a clinical (psychoanalytic) social work orientation could, under certain circumstances, have detrimental effects upon F.A.S. staff's ability to adapt themselves to the needs and purposes of this service.[3]

5. It appears that the key concepts, 'prevention' and 'advice', have not been uniformly or clearly defined. It seems that this lack of adequate conceptual thinking, is one of the main reasons for some degree of uncertainty, and for a considerable range of divergent opinions, regarding the goals and functions of the Family Advice Service.[4]

6. The impression was gained that the greatest proportion of F.A.S. clients comes from the working class and lower class population groups (manual, semi and unskilled labourers, unemployed or unemployable, etc.) and from the lower socio-economic strata of immigrant population groups.[5] This impression is *not* based on statistical evidence.

7. It appears that in the range of problems presented by F.A.S. clients, the following categories are regarded as predominant in the departments we visited:

a. Child rearing problems.
b. Marital conflict.

---

[1] For a more detailed discussion see Chapter 3, pp. 13–17 and Chapter 4, pp. 44–45
[2] For further details see Chapter 2, p. 5.
[3] Discussion of this subject can be found in Chapter 6, pp. 73–74.
[4] See Chapter 4, pp. 18–55.
[5] Ibid., p. 28.

c. Debts.

d. Inadequate housing.[1]

Again, this impression is *not* based on statistical evidence.

8. Generally speaking it seemed that, in most areas we visited, F.A.S. staff had a considerable measure of success in initiating and maintaining a type of 'grass-roots' co-ordination with the field staff of other statutory, local and voluntary agencies.[2]

9. The adequate staffing of F.A.S. units poses problems in many Children's Departments. In most cases trained staff cannot be made available in sufficient numbers. Furthermore, there is, as yet, no general agreement on the type of worker who would be most suitable for F.A.S. work.[3]

10. The practical experience of F.A.S. staff seems to underline the importance of consistent professional supervision in this special setting. It appears that the majority of the departments we visited have not solved the problem of adequate supervision.[4]

11. In many of the departments adequate and consistent recording appeared to be lacking.[5]

12. A considerable degree of concern was found among staff regarding possible duplications of functions of the Family Advice Service on the one hand, and the Children's Departments *per se*, on the other.[6]

There is even greater concern over possible duplications of functions between F.A.S. work and the services offered by other statutory, local and voluntary agencies.[7] The possibility, and the actual occurrence, of duplication and overlap seems to be most pronounced in the case of the Citizens' Advice Bureau.[8]

13. The problem of actual and potential conflict between the functions of the Family Advice Service and the statutory duties of Children's Department staff has aroused much discussion. Opinions on this issue are divided. Many practitioners feel that existing ambiguities in this area may affect the 'image' of the Family Advice Service. This issue seems to demand a policy decision.[9]

[1] See Chapter 4, p. 37.
[2] Ibid., pp. 52–55.
[3] See Chapter 5, pp. 57–58.
[4] See Chapter 5, p. 58–59.
[5] Ibid., pp. 59–60.
[6] Ibid., pp. 61–64.
[7] Ibid., pp. 64–70.
[8] Ibid., p. 70.
[9] Ibid., p. 70.

14. There is a great degree of interest in the future of the Family Advice Service among field and senior staff of the departments. In a number of the Children's Departments we visited, concrete plans for the future operation of new F.A.S. units, and for the improvement of existing services, are under consideration at the present time.[1]

Much thought is being given to the place of the operation of Family Advice Services within the framework of a unified Family Service, which is expected to emerge as a result of the recommendations of the Seebohm Committee.[2]

In the context of future planning, our observations indicate a need for the careful consideration of the kind of professional training which would be most suitable for F.A.S. work, and which would be most likely to provide staff with the necessary knowledge and information for this type of social work.[3]

15. Every aspect of the study points to the need for more factual information regarding the desirability of a Family Advice Service, the practical experience gathered within the various F.A.S. settings and the general and specific effects of F.A.S. work.[4] Not the least reason for this is the need, expressed in all the departments, to know more about the experience of F.A.S. in other departments, and to obtain specific data on the methods used, and the results achieved by them.

On the basis of this enquiry, it can be stated with some confidence that the present development of the Family Advice Services is, on the whole, an encouraging one (if it can be assumed that the sixteen Children's Departments we observed provide a representative picture of the country). Without ignoring the many problems and ambiguities which became apparent, we feel that our findings show that much useful work is being done, and that the concepts of the Family Advice Service and the commitment of all levels of staff to applying these concepts, offer a wide range of potentialities for a more effective and more efficient preventive social service approach. Realistic, practice-oriented research into the many facets and possibilities of Family Advice Services is essential for the eventual realisation of potentialities.

However, we are well aware that research alone will not answer all our questions. Sooner or later a number of fundamental issues will have to be faced which concern the basic tenets of social welfare. In the context of this study such issues cannot be dealt with in a manner which

[1] See Chapter 6, pp. 71–72.
[2] Ibid., p. 72.
[3] Ibid., pp. 73–74.
[4] See Chapter 7, pp. 76–78.

would do them justice. It must suffice here to reiterate the importance of these questions.

One of the first questions which suggests itself is, what scope can be allowed in practice to the concept of 'prevention', a concept that is fundamental to the tasks of the Family Advice Services? Are there limits set to its scope by the right of people to be left alone? How does our view on such limits affect our thinking on what the American social work practitioners call 'aggressive casework'?[1]

The problem of the detection of children and families 'at risk' is closely related to this issue,[2] as well as the complexities of the conflict between F.A.S. functions and statutory obligations.[3]

At this point we must consider the issue of 'permissiveness' versus the obligation to uphold and, where necessary, to help enforce, conformity with society's prescribed norms and values. The practitioner's own values come into the picture here. Moreover, while it may be assumed that a great degree of 'permissiveness' is essential if we want to establish the F.A.S. image as an easily accessible, 'safe' and unconditionally confidential service, we must ask whether it may not be confusing, or even harmful, for people *not* to be called to account when they transgress the norms of society, or when they fail to fulfil the obligations society imposes.[4]

These questions have, among others, led practitioners to ask whether the Family Advice Service should, indeed, operate under the auspices of a statutory agency, such as the Children's Department.[5] This, in turn, brings up the question of the division of labour between voluntary and statutory agencies in the modern Welfare State, which has recently become the subject of much discussion.

The question whether people should, at all, be induced to seek help and to make the widest possible use of the existing social services[6] is highly relevant to the 'prevention' concept, and, perhaps, even poses the question as to how far the basic tenets of 'institutionalised' social welfare have been assimilated, and to what degree 'residual' (or 'charity') concepts still influence our thinking.

These, and many other, questions must be answered. They should and do, play an important role in our search for the most effective and

[1] See in this context Chapter 4, p. 24, 'How aggressive should the Family Advice Service be?'.
[2] See Chapter 4, pp. 26–27.
[3] See Chapter 5, pp. 64–70.
[4] This too seems highly relevant to the problem of possible conflict between F.A.S. functions and statutory obligations.
[5] See Chapter 5, p. 61.
[6] This issue is touched upon in Chapter 4, pp. 46, 49 of the Study.

efficient ways and means of providing advice, guidance and assistance to all who are in need of help and support.

Needless to say, we cannot afford the luxury of waiting for the answers to all our questions, and for the solution of all our problems, before we get to work. A certain degree of pragmatism is essential, and the present work of the Family Advice Services is, indeed, a pragmatic attempt to find answers, while meeting the existing needs as well and as far as possible. The (in our opinion justified) optimism regarding the future development of F.A.S. can perhaps best be summed up in the words of field workers, who remarked, in conversation with the Research Officer:

'The Family Advice Service may very well become the wide open front door of our whole, big social service structure – F.A.S. could serve as the eyes and ears of the social service system, helping us to see where the needs are, and to hear what the people have to tell us.'

Bibliography

(Titles in order of reference in the text)

The Children and Young Persons Act, 1963, Introduction and annotations by Robert Schloss, Butterworth, London, 1964.

OXFORDSHIRE COUNTY COUNCIL, *Report of the Secretary of State under Section I (4) Children and Young Persons Act, 1963*, September 1964.

Joint Report by the Town Clerk, Medical Officer of Health, Housing Manager, Chief Welfare Officer, and Children's Officer of the London Borough of Camden General Purposes Committee, 3 February 1965.

Home Office Memorandum on the Reports of Local Authorities, 1 October 1963–31 July 1964.

Children's Officer's Report on the Family Advice Centre, Barrow-in-Furness Children's Department, 1964.

Cambridge House Annual Report, London Borough of Southwark, 1965.

Factual Memorandum by the Home Office on the Local Authority Children's Service in England and Wales, February 1966.

'Wait and See', *New Society*, 8 September 1966.

Evidence to the Committee on Local Authority and Allied Social Services, The Association of Children's Officers, April 1966.

BARBARA J. KAHAN, *The Work of the Children's Care Committee and the Children's Department*, Oxfordshire County Council, May 1965.

Home Office Circular No. 96, 1 June 1966.

ALFRED J. KAHN *et al.*, *Neighbourhood Information Centres*, Columbia University School of Social Work, New York, 1966.

HARLEIGH B. TRECKER, ed. *Group Work Foundations and Frontiers*, Whiteside Inc., New York 1955.

GISELA KONOPKA, *Social Group Work*, Prentice-Hall, Englewood, N.J., 1963.

A Family Service and a Family Court, by a Study Group of the Council for Children's Welfare, London.

A.C.C.O.'s *Evidence to Seebohm*, London, May 1966.

SHEILA M. KAY, 'The Future Development of Family Casework in the Non-Statutory Social Services', *Social Casework*, July 1966.

'Commentary', *Social Service Quarterly*, Autumn 1966.

M. L. KELLMER PRINGLE, ed. *Investment in Children*, Longmans, 1965.

BARBARA J. KAHAN, 'The Child, the Family, and the Young Offender', *British Journal of Criminology*, April 1966, p. 164.

MARGOT JEFFERYS, *Anatomy of Social Welfare Services*, Michael Joseph, London, 1965.

Proceedings of the Fifteenth Annual Conference of the Association of Children's Officers, Oxford, 1964.

E. HEIMLER, *Experiments in Community Care, the Hounslow Project*, July 1966.